What Your Fellow Badass Travelers Are Saying About *In Charge*

Since I am advocating for breaking rules that don't make sense to us, I'm taking my own advice and breaking the rule of what endorsements for a book should look like and who they should be from. These are endorsements from real women who read the book and felt that it was worth their time. I am humbled by and grateful for their endorsements, and I could not think of voices more esteemed to comment on this book than fellow badass travelers on this journey. —A.R.

"Arin doesn't know me. She doesn't know my struggles or what my day-to-day looks like. However, in just the first few pages alone, I feel like she sees ME. It was as if she sees that, despite the constant challenges I'm up against, I am not complaining or looking for sympathy...but that once in a while, it would be nice to not feel so f-ing exhausted at the end of the day. I don't want to hear "go for a massage," or "make time for yourself"—I know all that...and I wish it was that easy. This book has helped me reassess where my energy sucks are, and how take charge of how and where I focus my energy so that I don't feel like a total hot mess ALL. THE. TIME. Just the simple concept of "self-awareness," in the context that Arin dives into, has helped make a world of a difference in finding—and hopefully sustaining—my peace. I only say "hopefully" because there is 42 years of "not knowing any differently" that I need to adjust and work on—which is why I will definitely be re-reading this book, and all my highlights and notes again and again."
—*Sharon*

"Thank you so much for sharing these powerful and refreshingly honest stories. I have never felt so seen and understood. I laughed out loud and cried tears of relief. I feel like I have finally found my tribe, and have permission to be unapologetically me—to speak up, subtract, say no, and yes, even curse and touch the controls (not that I needed permission)!"
—*Angelique*

"Imagine being guided to breaking the rules, finding your reset button and claiming your safe space while expressing yourself as strongly as you choose. You will find all of that in *In Charge*, shared in a way that is about real women and real situations and that comes from the heart of an author who brings her personal experiences as well as the data to prove her points. Through her new book, Arin Reeves charts the course for women to peace, joy and acknowledgment—with energy to spare and supported by a community of strong women. I couldn't stop highlighting—there were so many parts I wanted to remember!"
—*Mary Ellen*

"NEVER QUIT, BUT STOP WHAT ISN'T WORKING" needs to be on a billboard. This statement resonates with me so well. I've always been the hustler, the go-getter, the to-do lister. I set a goal, I achieve it—but never realize how much pressure I put on myself to achieve it until life smacks me upside the head to remind me. The "1 out, 1 in" rule has been a game changer for me. I've incorporated it into current passion projects I'm working on and WOW, I've noticed the difference. I'm learning that I can do it all, but not all at once and not at the cost of my physical and mental health."
—*Jennifer*

"I don't have time to read books. I have more unread books at home than books that have even been opened. When Arin asked me to read this book and give her a couple of sentences for the back of the book if I wanted to I said yes—but I didn't expect to be able to get to it. I picked it up and couldn't put it down. I read several parts out loud with my sister. The book was not what I expected it to be, but it was honestly exactly what I needed to read right now. All of it resonated, but if I had to pick just one thing to recommend to you? *Hell yes to the chapter on cursing.*"
—*Michelle*

"Read the book. Do the exercises. I don't know you but I know it will be worth your time."
—*Janice*

"Holy shit! I've seen Arin Reeves in her trainings and workshops, and she's hilarious. She manages to write the way she presents. This book felt like a conversation with a good friend—you know, that friend that you call who will call you out on your shit and make you feel loved at the same time. I will be sharing this book with the women in my life and talking about it with them."
—*Samara*

"I saw myself in so many of the women's stories. Different parts of myself. This book is wise and sarcastic in equal parts. You can feel Arin's passion for empowering women. Anna's story resonated with me because of my own experiences. It was heavy. And the epilogue to that story? Fucking priceless. Definitely worth your time and money, many times over."
—*Margo*

"Dang it girl, you made me cry! And laugh. And get pissed off. And feel hugged. Loved the section on celebrating, and the exercises were easy to follow and powerful."
—*Lynne*

"I was one of the women Arin interviewed for this book. Reading my own story made me realize how much progress I've made since I started working with her. But reading the other stories made me realize I was not alone in my struggles. This book is your reminder that you are not alone in what you are experiencing, and that we can make a difference for ourselves in our lives and for other women too."

—*Gina*

"Okay, the story about the chimpanzee cursing made me laugh out loud on the train. When the woman sitting a couple of seats from me looked up I told her about the book and read some of the chimpanzee story to her. We laughed hysterically the rest of the ride. I read her more from the book and she took down Arin's information and said that she couldn't wait to get the book. She and I have stayed in touch. That's the power of women sharing stories."

—*Sonia*

"I loved the book and I'm excited to share it with my friends. I'm even more excited to share it with my daughter and her friends who are in their mid-twenties. I wish I had read something like this before I started following a truckload of rules that I am now needing to break."

—*Kiersten*

"Pissedoffness is my new favorite word. Who the fuck knew that one word could capture so much of life right now. I love it. I love that Arin can make a topic like exhaustion and pissedoffness fun to read. She talks about joy in this book. The book was a joy to read."

—*Yara*

In Charge

The Energy Management Guide for Badass Women
Who Are Tired of Being Tired

Dr. Arin N. Reeves

For media inquiries, questions about bulk purchases, permission to use any of the content of this book, or speaking availability, please visit www.ArinReeves.com.

Library of Congress CIP is on file.

ISBNs:
978-1-7330647-6-7 (hardcover)
978-1-7330647-7-4 (ebook)

ZRI
PUBLISHING

to caelan and miles
for your courage to be true to yourselves
as you discover yourselves

Table of Contents

ACTIONS TO GET IN CHARGE

Gratitude

There are years that ask questions and years that answer.
—Zora Neale Hurston
Their Eyes Were Watching God

I am deeply grateful for the years in my life that had more questions than answers because those years helped me grow. I am deeply grateful for the years in my life that gave me answers to my questions even when the answers hurt like hell because those years helped me heal.

Writing is an exercise in solitude, but writing and publishing a book can only happen with a community of people who believe in you enough to push you out of solitude into creating something that can be shared with the world. I know this book would not have become a reality without the inspiring, brilliant, determined, and loving community that helped me through and throughout the last few years.

Caelan and Miles, just wow. As a writer, it is humbling to admit that I don't have the words to describe how in awe I am of both of you. Caelan, your wicked sense of humor combined with your sharp ass mind and even sharper courage amaze me every day. You were born a badass, and even when you don't feel like the badass you are, your badassness radiates for the world to see. I'm grateful for your smile, your wisdom, and your friendship more than I could adequately express. Miles, you are such a beautiful balance of confidence and humility, brilliance and bullshit, ambitious and carefree. You are an empathetic soul with a warrior's spirit. You are also one hell of a road trip buddy and a phenomenal teacher of all things cars and crypto. I have no idea how the two of you manage to bounce from wise old souls to wise asses in the blink of an eye, but this world is a better place because the two of you are in it. I am a better person because the two of you are in my life.

SHSC, could 2021 have been a crazier year? The three of you held me tight through some of the darkest moments of my life and kicked my ass when I needed (and, uhm, even when I didn't need it?) because you wanted me to create the life I wanted to live. You have made me a smarter thinker, a better writer, and a stronger person. How do I just say thank you? How am I ever going to fully convey that I would not be thriving if it weren't for you?

To each badass woman who gave me permission to tell your story in this book, a storyteller is only as good as the stories they tell. This book shines because you shine, and I am so grateful for everything each of you taught, inspired, and gifted me.

Tim, you have stuck with me and pushed me through four books now. You know you are stuck with me and my crazy ideas, right? You have trusted me to follow my truths and you have helped me create books from ideas. Every time I have finished a book, I am in a mild state of shock that it's actually done. Thank you for your patience, your insights, your guidance, and most of all your friendship.

To everyone on the Nextions team who read the drafts, stretched my thinking, and kept me on track, thank you thank you thank you. Emma, a special thank you to you. You stepped in and kept me going through the rough times of January and February (aka the crazy codeine months!)

There are so many more of you for whom I'm so grateful. I plan to spend the next few months telling you personally...with the requisite drinks, cursing, and hugging that conveys the full depth of my gratitude!

To each of the women who read the early drafts of this and help me make it better and to the women who read the drafts and gave me blurbs to share with the world, thank you!

I am grateful for those whose shoulders I stand on and for those whose wisdom flows through me. I am grateful for the magical wordsmiths whose works inspire me every day and remind me that words are a powerful path through which ancient truths can be woven into our modern lives.

And, I am ever grateful to every reader who deems this book worthy of their most precious resource – their time – and I hope you feel love and hope I have for you as you create a life that brings you peace and joy.

Onward,
Arin

INTRODUCTION

SHE IS YOU
SHE IS ME
SHE IS US

She is a badass woman.

Even if she doesn't feel like it every day. Especially when she doesn't feel like it. She gets up and kicks ass anyway because she doesn't have a choice. She is strong, and often much stronger than those around her. She loves that she can help others, but she also wishes they would get their shit together so she doesn't have to do it for them.

She's a daughter, a mom, an aunt, a sister, a wife, a partner, an ex-wife, a friend, a lover, a teacher, a student, a colleague, a leader, a fighter, a peacemaker, a healer, and so much more, and often all at once. She's a pain in the ass to those who deserve it, and a fierce warrior for those who need it. She has learned that she can be exhausted and inspired at the same time, just as she can love someone and want to slap some sense into them at the same time.

She is kind but not always nice, because she's exhausted. She's compassionate but not a pushover, though she often lets herself get pushed over because she needs her energy for other things in that moment and for the future battles that she knows await her. She knows the difference between giving up and letting go but she also knows that letting go is so much harder than giving up. It pisses her off when she is seen as giving up when she did the hard work it took to let go.

She's not afraid to be herself but she doesn't believe that everyone deserves (or can handle) who she really is. She has been told she's too loud, too strong, too ambitious, too determined, too much, and she wonders why any of that is bad, but she has learned to "tone it down" to survive. She knows how much energy it takes to not roll her eyes or slam the table with her fists when she is interrupted by people who have no idea what they are talking about. She knows how much energy it takes to swallow the words she needs to say in her defense because if she did say them, she would be called defensive. She knows how to dim her light, bend her will, mute her voice, pause her fight, and soften her gaze to make room for the insecurities and fears of others, because she cannot afford the price that she will pay for being brighter, stronger, and more powerful than those with the insecurities and fears.

She's infinitely patient when she makes herself heard for the first time and rightfully impatient when she has to repeat herself...over and over again. She makes space for other people's weaknesses and excuses even though she is not always given the space to be weak or to make excuses. She is soft and hard, comfortable and uncomfortable in the dualities she negotiates every day. She manages chaos she did not create and cleans up messes she did not make. She's not happy about it, but she knows complaining will only deplete energy she does not have to spare.

People may not always know when they piss her off, but she will never forget the who, what, when, where, and why. She cares about candor more than propriety and is weighed down by how often she needs to choose propriety over candor. She has been told that she should choose her battles, but she doesn't always know how to do that when there are so many battles she faces every day, battles that threaten her sanity, peace, and joy.

She doesn't get over being hurt, she absorbs the hurt to make herself stronger. She doesn't get over being pissed off, she absorbs the pissedoffness to use as fuel for her journey. She takes the big blows and wins and the small cuts and victories and blends them together into her unique brand of grace and mettle, a brand that is as powerful as it is weary.

She is exactly who you want beside you in a crisis. She is loyal even when it goes against her best interests, but once she decides someone no longer deserves her loyalty, they should watch their backs...probably for the rest of their lives. She has no use for revenge, but she will never give up on justice. She has been told many times that she is too angry, so she has learned how to smile through her anger. But those who deserve her just anger should be afraid, especially when she is smiling.

She's not afraid to break the rules, but she breaks rules to create order, not chaos.

Did I mention that she's exhausted? Is there any doubt as to why?

She is not alone. She has women in her life who have her back, sisters who make the space for her to break down, who tell her to get back in the game when the time for tears is over. And if she doesn't, she knows that she is the strongest advocate she has on her side. She knows how to wipe her own tears just as well as she knows how to console others.

She is the badass woman in other women's lives—and in her own life when necessary, not because she feels a sense of obligation but because that is just who she is. And has always been.

She knows how talented she is, and she knows that she will not always be recognized for her contributions because she doesn't have the time, the energy, or the space to jump up and down and whine for credit. There are a lot of things she doesn't speak up about, not because she's afraid but because too many people have convinced her of their inability to understand. She's not arrogant, but she knows there are many people in positions of power who are just idiots with great self-promotion skills.

She has been underestimated more times than she can count, and she has also transformed that underestimation into a superpower more times than she can count. She has been pushed around, pushed down, and pushed out, but she is still fighting every day.

She knows many books have been written about how she should be more ambitious and confident, how she should lean in, how she should better balance her life and work, and how she should do all of this with glowing skin, a toned body, perfectly coiffed hair, and a wide-ass smile. She reads them all (or at least quick summaries of them online) and consciously feels like they are full of shit and unconsciously wonders what's wrong with her and why she just can't pull it all together. These books have been written about her but not always for her, because there is actually nothing wrong with her. There is nothing about her that needs fixing.

This book is written for her, this badass woman living in this twenty-first-century world with all of its freedoms, constrictions, expectations, limitations, celebrations, pains, successes, and disappointments. She navigates them all with equal—or unequal—parts grace, joy, determination, anger, and exhaustion.

This book is written for her...and by her.

She is you. She is me. She is us.

As a fellow traveler, I have gathered hundreds of stories of her journeys, and this book is an homage to her energy, resilience, passion, kindness, courage, and creativity. This book honors her deep exhaustion and her powerful spirit. It is also a conversation among sisters who may not know each other but who have much to share with each other about ways to be in charge of our lives in a world that doesn't always make it easy to do so.

I have written other books as a researcher, but I write this book as a fellow traveler, a fellow traveler who fought my own battles as I tried to capture our collective dance through the muck. I don't have all the answers, but I have learned that we badass women have figured it out more than we give ourselves credit for.

This badass woman is you, me, the women we lean on when the most important things are on the line, the women we are raising, and the women we honor as trailblazers who made it a little easier for those of us who came after them. This badass woman doesn't need help with how to do her job, raise her kids, lead her community, have her friends' backs, or keep her family better connected. She doesn't need help being confident, ambitious, brilliant, or anything else.

She needs acknowledgment that she is kicking ass in a world that's not set up to work for her.

She needs to know that she is not alone in feeling exhausted, frustrated, pissed off, unsupported, etc. etc. etc.

This book is that message of acknowledgment. It is also the gathering of our collective wisdom on how to make this journey

less exhausting and frustrating and _____
(please fill in whatever word(s) feel most relevant in this moment for you). Or draw a picture, because sometimes words are just not enough.

To each of the women who trusted me with their stories, I am more grateful than I could ever express. Even if I had not written this book, your stories inspired and empowered me to get and be more in charge of my own life.

Thank you, and onward!

A REFLECTION
FOR MY SISTERS
IN THE MARGINS

purposefully stayed away from overfocusing on the race/ethnicity, sexual orientation, neurodiversity, socioeconomic condition, physical or other disabilities and other identity aspects of women whose stories enliven this book. I believe that the insights from the stories are applicable to any woman that can benefit from them. That said, I am painfully aware of how the lives and experiences of women who navigate the challenges in the margins have dimensions of complexity, frustration, pain, and exhaustion that extend beyond what is faced by women who don't navigate those same challenges.

I struggled with the decision to not make these marginalized identities a larger part of the narratives. On one hand, these identities were part of how women saw themselves and their experiences. On the other hand, the marginalized identities were experienced so differently by each woman based on the other identities she was navigating in her life in that moment that I felt focusing on these identities clouded more than clarified the core issue in each woman's story. Where it was important to the woman that I include it, I included it. Where it wasn't, I left it out.

As a woman of color who is a first-generation immigrant to this country, I know firsthand the challenges of experiencing life at the intersection of race and gender. But, when I've shared my story with white women who were born and raised here, there were many parts of my narrative that they resonated with. There were many strategies that worked for me that worked for them too. Similarly, as a straight woman, I've connected deeply with and learned from the experiences of gay women. Some of my strategies as a mom have worked powerfully for clients of mine who don't have children, and I've adopted some great ideas from them that work for clients of mine who are raising children.

When early readers of this manuscript did not know these identity aspects of the women they were reading about, they connected with stories they told me they wouldn't have connected with if they had known that the woman was a different race or sexual orientation from them. Unfortunately, this is the world in which we live today. Our differences divide us instead of being sources from which we can learn and grow.

Women in the margins are exhausted from describing their experiences and challenges. Women in the majority are uncomfortable approaching the conversations and terrified of getting it wrong. I didn't want to add to the crap we are all negotiating right now.

I've seen ideas for being in charge of our lives transcend age, profession, socioeconomic levels, personality types and so much more in addition to race, ethnicity, and sexual orientation. I wanted this book to be a reflection of that transcendence, an opportunity for every woman to see something that she could take and use from each story in these pages.

I made the choice to make this book as resonant and useful as possible for any woman who picked it up, but I made the choice with a heavy heart and conscience knowing that marginalized women experience not being in charge in ways that are intensely more difficult to describe and negotiate. Considering the distance we have to cover to go from not being in charge to being in charge is sometimes like looking into an abyss. Yet, it is precisely in these margins where I found the greatest resilience and most creative paths to peace, joy, acknowledgment, and community.

Women who navigate partially or wholly in the margins are exhausted in ways that we don't yet have the words to describe. Mental health issues abound in the margins as do challenges to getting the resources and support you need to navigate those issues. Not only are we living in a world that doesn't value us, but many of us are raising our children in a world that feels more dangerous to them by the day.

This is where I feel my fellow traveler role in my bones. I have mastered the art of crying and laughing at the same time just as I've mastered the art of crying with my sisters and making them laugh at the same time.

And, through it all, I still do believe that we women have more that connects us together than separates us. I still do believe that we can learn from each other and be unwavering sisters and allies in each other's communities. I know that others may disagree with me on this. There are some days where I disagree with myself on this.

I hope this book sparks conversations between us that help us erase enough of the margins to remind us that we don't always have to understand each other to have each other's backs.

SHE IS IN CHARGE &
SHE IS NOT IN CHARGE

March 2009

I was exhausted.

I had been traveling two or three times a week for months on end. Most of the trips were grueling day trips with flights departing Chicago before 6:00 a.m. and returning to Chicago any time between 7 p.m. and 2 a.m. These "day trips" were my "choice," a.k.a., the only way I could travel for work and still be present for my 5-year-old daughter and my 3-year-old son, whose fourth birthday was in a few days.

I knew I was exhausted. But I was so incredibly grateful to have the opportunity to do the work I did. I was changing how workplaces worked, especially for women, people of color and other people from underrepresented communities. I was coaching people to be stronger and more resilient in their career journeys.

I was hearing from people every day that the work I was doing was making a difference in their workplaces and for them personally, so I was okay with being exhausted. Actually, I thought that being exhausted was just part of doing the work of equity and inclusion. Sometimes I even equated the exhaustion with the depth of my commitment to create positive change.

I remember waking up one day in March 2009, thinking I had a really bad cold. My head was pounding. I couldn't breathe easily. I felt feverish. But I got up, got dressed, made breakfast for the kids, took them to their respective schools, and went to work feeling not fully like my usual self but ready to do my calls, prep for a presentation that evening at a client's office, and finish some research for a cognitive biases article that was due in a couple of days.

Within a couple of hours after I got to the office, my head was hurting so badly that I could barely think. I started feeling chilled to the bone and I was shivering uncontrollably, even though I was cocooned in multiple layers of sweaters in my exceptionally warm office. I felt terrible, and I decided that if I was going to make my presentation that evening, I needed to cancel the rest of my calls for the day and get some rest. I remember getting into bed. I remember calling my babysitter and asking her to pick up the kids from school. I remember thinking that my presentation was about four hours away, and if I could just sleep for a couple of hours, I would be fine.

I'm sure you guessed by now that it didn't work out the way I thought it would. I don't remember much after I got into bed. I woke up in the emergency room many hours later to the worried face of a nurse. I asked her where my kids were, and I tried to get up. She gently pushed me back down and told me that I had a fever north of 104 degrees.

A very stern-faced physician came in a few minutes later and told me that I had pneumonia and that my right lung was almost fully collapsed. He told me that my primary care doctor had been called and was on his way. The X-rays looked bad and something about my oxygenation was even worse, but I couldn't focus on what he was saying. My mind was racing. *What day is it? What time is it? Where are my kids? Are they okay? How did I get here? Aren't I supposed to be somewhere for work?*

When my primary care doctor arrived, he studied my chart before saying anything to me. When he finally looked at me, he sighed loudly and shook his head dramatically. "Do you have any idea how ill you are?" he asked me. It was all I could do to not roll my eyes at him. "I'm sure you are about to tell me," I answered.

He frowned at me and told me that I had clearly been very sick for a long time and that I, *a mother*, should know better than to put off getting the medical attention I should have known I needed. Yes, he actually said that. He glared at me like I should have felt some shame, at the very least a little contrition, given that I was in the emergency room with oxygen support. I searched for shame and contrition but found none. Instead, I found rage, a deep pissedoffness that made my bones hurt.

I wasn't sure why I was angry or at whom, but the pissedoffness intensified when my doctor admitted me and told me that he couldn't trust me to take care of myself at home. As he prepared my admission papers, I made some calls and was able to relax a little when I heard my kids' voices. I reached my assistant, who told me that my client and co-panelists—all of them women—had been understanding and compassionate. They'd asked her where they could send me flowers and asked her to tell me that I had prepared them well. I felt guilty for having let them down, and I was grateful for their kindness.

As I was being wheeled out of the emergency room toward my inpatient room, my doctor gave me another lecture on how I, a mother, should have known better, and I didn't have the energy to prevent myself from rolling my eyes sarcastically. But his words still got to me. I felt guilty about ending up in the hospital. I felt guilty about letting down my clients. I felt guilty that I wasn't at home for my kids. I felt all this guilt right alongside the growing pissedoffness the doctor was inspiring with his every word.

I was in my inpatient room buzzing with guilt anger and frustration. A nurse came in, introduced herself, read my chart, and frowned. "They don't usually admit people for this," she said. "But we'll do what we can to make you comfortable as the antibiotics do their work." I asked her what the usual course of treatment was for cases similar to mine. "Antibiotics, ibuprofen, sleep," she responded.

I left the hospital an hour later—against doctor's orders—armed with antibiotics, ibuprofen, and discharge papers where someone had emphatically written and underlined "Lots of rest and follow up with PCP in 2 days!"

I did get rest. I did get better. And, on my way to my follow-up appointment two days later, I told myself that the doctor could not have been as bad as I was remembering.

Alas, he was worse. He greeted me with more shaking of his head and told me how women today were just trying too hard to be too many things. He pontificated about how my pneumonia was caused by me, a working mother of two young children, doing too much and degrading my immune system. (The ironic use of the word degrading in this context deserves its own chapter!)

I asked him—sincerely—what I could be doing to make my immune system stronger, and he told me to...quit working. He said that he really believed women could not have it all and when women—like me—tried to have it all, we ended up in the hospital and unable to care for our children as they deserve. Yes, he actually said that.

Then, he wrote down "consider extended leave from employment" as his recommended course of treatment.

Needless to say, I found myself a new primary care physician. A couple of simple tests ordered by my new female physician identified that I had several vitamin deficiencies and other fixable issues that helped me recover from the pneumonia relatively quickly and also strengthened my immune system.

I felt better, but I was not less pissed off. I couldn't shake the feeling that I had experienced something unfair and disrespectful, but I couldn't articulate exactly what it was. As I felt better, the researcher in me got to work.

I started talking to people I knew—men and women—about health crises in their lives and how they had dealt with them. I asked people what advice they had received from medical professionals and what they had done to recalibrate their lives to get and stay healthy. A pattern slowly emerged from these conversations:

▷ Almost all the women had heard some version of "you should quit your job, you can't possibly take care of yourself and your family, and thrive in your career" without any consideration to the specifics of their personal, family, or financial lives, and

▷ Almost all the men had heard some version of "delegate more work, ask your family to better understand your stress and how much your work requires of you, and get more support to from everyone in your life" without any consideration to the specifics of their personal, family, or financial lives.

▷ None of the women who heard that they should quit their jobs heard anything about their families stepping up to support them, and none of the men who heard that they should get more support from their colleagues or families heard that they should quit or what additional stressors would be experienced by the people who they were seeking support from.

Of course, this was not the experience of every woman or every man who shared their stories with me, but the overall patterns were irritatingly clear.

The anger buzzing in my brain started to make more sense. Underneath the lopsided recommendations was a fundamental assumption: work was a necessity for men, but work was a choice for women. *If something is a necessity, you figure out how to deal with the challenges that arise because quitting isn't an option. But if something is a choice you are making, challenges that arise are a signal for you to make a different choice.*

And swimming just beneath these assumptions of work as a necessity or a choice were other assumptions of how the people who were making the "choice" to work—women—were also making the "choice" to neglect their families, and the people for whom "work" was a necessity—men—were not only doing right by their families but that maybe they were sick because their families—women—weren't supportive enough. None of the women heard anything about asking their families to be more supportive.

I thought back to how often my doctor had said "as a mother" as he had chided me. I wondered what he said to fathers. I wondered if he realized how he was insisting that I was in charge of taking care of my kids and that I was not in charge of taking care of myself at the same time.

I didn't have the option of quitting my job. Also, I didn't want to quit my job! I just wanted to find ways to do my job, be a kickass mom, and live my life...without pneumonia and lung collapses. Did the medical community or even society at large consider that so remote of a possibility that they couldn't help me figure out how to stay healthy and have a successful and meaningful working life?

What started as a journey in answering that question has morphed into a journey of collecting stories of women across the world who have been asking and creatively constructing answers to similar questions. Some of the stories will make you laugh, some will make you cringe, some will make you cry, some will make you angry, and some may even leave you not knowing how to react. But all the stories are insights into how women reached a boiling point in their lives and took actions to be "in charge" of their lives in spite of the circumstances that stretched them too thin, stressed them out, and just plain pissed them off.

This Book & Your In Charge Journey

> *We do not need, and indeed never will have,*
> *all the answers before we act...*
> *It is often through taking action*
> *that we can discover some of them.*
> *— Charlotte Bunch*

When I started researching energy management for women, I was frustrated that almost all of the research and resources were related to self-care, the "take time out for yourself, take more baths, go to the spa, get plenty of exercise, drink more water, take a walk in nature, start meditating" type of self-care. These types of self-care activities are important, but they don't address the energy depletion cycles that women are experiencing. They just make you feel a little better—a little more rested—in the moment, but the energy-depleting shit that activated the need for the bath, massage, nature walk, etc. is still there waiting for you when the self-care is over.

Imagine that you are on a large ship that has sprung a leak. The ship is not in danger of sinking immediately, so everything that needs to be done on the ship normally still needs to be done, but now you also have to bail out the water that's coming in from the leak. After a full day of working your ass off keeping the ship running as usual and bailing the accumulating water, you are exhausted and frustrated. Now imagine if someone saw how exhausted you were and suggested that you relax a little by taking a long hot bath. Of course, the bath sounds amazing. Of course, it feels good to enjoy the bath and not think about the work that still needs to get done or the water that still needs to be bailed. But when you get out of that bath, even if you go to sleep and get a good night's rest, all of what exhausted you today will be there waiting for you tomorrow. Energy management is as much about finding and patching that leak and getting everyone on that ship to step up to do what they are supposed to do as it is taking a long, hot bath at the end of the day and getting a good night's rest.

Interestingly, men's self-care tips include some of the same suggestions for exercise, hydration, and time in nature, but they also include recommendations for consuming good whiskeys, playing competitive sports like boxing and squash, and setting ambitious goals to boost their self-confidence. To evoke the ship metaphor again, men's self-care tips seem to reasonably expect stress and exhaustion at the end of working all day on a ship and bailing water, and they suggest ways in which the stress can be alleviated so that the exhaustion can be neutralized through rest. Whiskey and squash are great—until you're exhausted and working on a perpetually leaking ship. Then you need some actual help, and rest.

There are multiple disciplines and frameworks that approach personal energy management, including neurobiology, psychology, sociology, physics, physical health, mindfulness, wellness, time management, and work-life balance tools, to name just a few. All of these disciplines play a role in understanding how to get and stay in charge, but none can help you manage your energy deliberately all day, every day, so you can accomplish all you need to do. An interdisciplinary approach to energy management enables us to see all of the various influences we have to negotiate to efficiently use our energy.

The framework of energy management I use pulls all the various research disciplines together to understand your individual system, identify what order looks like and feels like in your system, recognize the internal and external causes of entropy, identify the mechanisms to restore order, and implement the most self-sustaining order-balancing processes to make sure that you are enjoying the heck out of living in your system. The simplified version is: identify what makes you happy, identify what pisses you off; then do less of what pisses you off and more of what makes you happy. Then you can set up your life to neutralize the bad stuff without much effort so that you can really enjoy the good stuff.

Sounds simple enough, but we all know that simple doesn't always mean easy. In our attempts to manage our energy more efficiently, to neutralize entropy, and restore order, we often run into some common energy drains that make it difficult for us to live the lives we really want to live.

These drains have multiple ways of showing up in our lives. Sometimes they show up as explicit rules in a particular context or as clear barriers preventing you from doing what you want to do. Other times, they may show up as unspoken expectations or subtle pressure to bend in a particular direction to avoid conflict or negative consequences. Everyone negotiates these drains, but the less you are in charge of how the sociocultural systems operate, the less able you are in being able to directly counteract the energy drains. The drains that the women I interviewed most frequently referred to were:

▷ Personal and professional ambitions, goals, and desires that you didn't choose

▷ Physical, cognitive, financial, and emotional health, habits, and cycles resulting from living in a way that you didn't choose

▷ Inadequate resources to manage physical, cognitive, financial, and emotional health, habits, and cycles

▷ Lack of control over physical location, living environment, and family/roommates who share the living space

▷ Social/cultural expectations at home and in family relationships that are misaligned with personal values and aspirations

▷ Social/cultural expectations in the workplace that are misaligned with personal values and aspirations

▷ Social/cultural expectations of friends and professional acquaintances that are misaligned with personal values and aspirations

▷ Social media and cultural media that create unrealistic expectations

▷ Seasonal changes and necessary access to different natural environments that impact all aspects of health

▷ Current events, political events, and sociopolitical impacts
to community that cannot be ignored

We will tackle these energy drains in this book, recognizing that we can't always slay them or make them go away. We will explore ways to minimize their impacts or create realistic ways to circumvent them.

This book synthesizes research from multiple disciplines to explore how you can get in charge and stay in charge of your life using practical and sustainable actions to neutralize energy drains. You will read real stories of how women explored the entropy in their lives and took actions to recover from burnout and create a life that worked for them and that made them happier. This book will also explore why the ability to deliberately direct your energy is most critical for people from groups underrepresented in social power structures and the role that energy management can play in increasing inclusion and equity in our workplaces and communities. It isn't that energy management principles change based on who you are, but that the management of energy is different based on what and how much you must negotiate, and which tools are available as resources for you.

This book started off as my own journey in trying to find and patch the energy leaks in my life, and I have been incredibly fortunate to connect with other women on the same journey who shared their lessons with me and empowered and encouraged me to share our collective insights with other women before they had to learn the lessons the hard way, as we did. As I researched, experimented, coached, and shared, the key ideas arranged themselves into the outline for this book.

An interesting pattern emerged in my interviews, coaching sessions, and conversations with women on how to be and feel in charge of their lives. Women would first start talking about how different their lives would be if their workplaces were different, if the rules were different, if they had more help with childcare, if they didn't have to continually walk that tightrope of being strong enough to be assertive without getting pushed into the bitch category, if business metaphors weren't immersed in sports, violence, or sexual innuendo, if...if...if. And then they would sigh, partially in quiet frustration and partially in acceptance. After the sigh and a moment of silence, I would ask them what they wanted to set as their intentions and aspirations—their reasons for doing this work of inner and outer change.

Initially, I was surprised at their answers. I expected the women to talk about advancing at work, achieving a bold new goal, starting a business, or something else related to these kinds of accomplishments. And although that's how the answers started out, but that's not how the answers ended. *I want to start my own business so that I can be more myself every day. I want to make partner so that I can be more in control of my own schedule. I want to get into a leadership position so that I can help more women succeed. I want to exceed my sales goals so that I can work from home more without people bugging me about why I'm not in the office. I want to travel more and be able to unplug when I do. I want to be able to be present for my kids. I want to reconnect with my friends. I want more time to volunteer for causes I care about. I want to be able to work hard and play hard without worrying about justifying how I spend my time.*

The more these stories began to crystallize into a cohesive and consistent pattern, the more I began to worry about potential biases in my subject-selection process, self-selection errors in my coaching clients (would people who chose me as their coach be more likely to fall into these pattens?), and my interview style. I reached out to a few male and female coaches to see what they were hearing from their female clients, and the stories their clients were telling were very similar to the stories I was hearing. I decided to do a small experiment: I asked a few of my clients/subjects to select one woman in their lives who was different from them on at least four of the following eight demographic identities—race/ethnicity, gender, generation, socioeconomic status, sexual orientation, educational level, geographical region (not in the same state, at least), and religious beliefs/affiliations—and ask them what they wanted more of in their lives and what was preventing them for getting/having what they wanted.

This nonscientific detour in the research revealed even more stories that confirmed the pattern I was observing. The collective impact of the stories overwhelmed me, and every time I sat down to summarize or analyze or write, I found myself agitated and upset in ways I couldn't define. I would set time aside to do this work, and I would inevitably do something else. A few weeks went by without me moving forward. The weeks turned into three months.

I was having drinks with one of my friends one evening while I was in the throes of not writing, and I lamented about the guilt I felt for not meeting my deadlines.

"Are you just too busy to be working on this book right now?" she asked me.

"No," I answered honestly. "I make the time, but I am not processing the women's stories like I usually process narrative data. I'm sitting with these stories for a long time. I'm writing and rewriting without feeling like I'm capturing all that I want to capture."

Then she asked if I was having trouble processing the infor-mation and writing the book because I was trying to process and write about the same experiences I was navigating in my own life.

I wrestled with that question for a few days, and I did what no researcher should ever do: I interviewed myself. My own responses fit the maddeningly cohesive pattern. I was both the researcher and a subject, a narrator and a story. I wasn't writing objectively about the journeys that women were taking to be in charge of their lives. I was a fellow traveler writing about stories in this collective journey that I was living and studying simultaneously.

My realization agitated my inner critic. *A researcher can't be in the study, right? That's definitely not allowed. What genre would this book be? People didn't want to read about my life. They wanted to read the research. It wouldn't be right to just do a book about women. Shouldn't I do more research on men and make this book gender neutral? This will never work. People will lose respect for me as a researcher, won't they?* My inner critic always has a lot to say, and she yapped insistently for several days on this specific subject.

I wrote. I stopped. I got frustrated again because I wasn't writing. I left the book alone to be present with my children as their education moved into the virtual world. At the same time, I led my firm and clients through the disruption of the pandemic and the challenge of working in justice, equity, diversity, and inclusion during the racial justice uprising in the summer of 2020, and the maniacally crazy presidential election.

I started and stopped writing so many times that I found myself wondering if I needed to abandon this book altogether. But I kept coming back to it, getting a little more clarity each time, writing a little more confidently as I applied the lessons learned to intense challenges I was facing in my own life.

This book was shaped by my lived experiences of the insights contained in it as much as it was informed by my research. To paraphrase Elizabeth Gilbert, this book is a glorious mess of a lot of things that may not go together on first glance, but that come together in a strangely cohesive way to teach us how to step into being the badass women we really are.

I honestly don't know if my inner critic just got tired or if I stopped listening to her, or if the need to write *this* book overrode the need to write a neatly organized, easily explainable book, but one day I woke up at peace with the messiness of it all. I am a fellow traveler writing about a journey that I'm living, experimenting with, learning from, changing, and writing simultaneously.

In Charge: A Definition

Energy cannot be created or destroyed.
It can only be changed from one form to another.
—*Albert Einstein*

Energy is defined by physicists as the amount of work a physical system can perform. Energy cannot be created or consumed or destroyed, but it can be transformed from one type of energy to another. We will stay in the very shallow end of the physics pool and not dive too deeply into all the various forms of energy, but a basic grounding in what energy is and how it works is useful in helping us understand how we choose to use it to live our lives. For example, potential energy in your resting body can be transformed into the kinetic energy of motion, and kinetic energy can be transformed into thermal energy to increase the temperature of our bodies. If we think of ourselves as individual physical systems, we can see that we have a finite amount of energy that we can expend each day to live our lives. We cannot create new energy or destroy the energy we have, but by efficiently transforming the energy from one necessary form to another as we need to, we create positive lived experiences that are consistent with how we want to live our lives. When we are inefficient at transforming the energy in our lives into the necessary forms we need that day, we experience exhaustion, frustration, and other negative lived experiences.

Along with this framework for energy, physics also gives us a framework for understanding how energy breaks down order in a system—entropy. Entropy is the amount of disorder in any system. You can think of disorder as anything that works against how you reasonably define order. For example, if you think about a kitchen as a functional system, there are dishes and utensils in that kitchen for people to use to consume their food. Each time a dish or piece of silverware is used, there is a bit of disorder. It needs to be cleaned so it can go back into the orderly rotation of being available for use. If dishes aren't washed, and they continue to pile up in the sink, you will eventually run out of usable dishes, you won't be able to use the sink, and the system will have a high level of entropy. Every time the dishes are washed and put away, the entropy is neutralized, and order is restored. In almost all systems—especially human systems—the system will default to disorder because it takes energy to restore order. (It takes less energy to let dishes pile up than it does to wash them regularly.) And the disorder in the system will increase over time unless order is deliberately and consistently restored. This process of reversing entropy is negentropy; it is the increase of order in a system, which counters the natural disorder that builds over time.

The cognitive psychologist and computational brain theorist Steven Pinker summarized the dynamic this way: "The ... ultimate purpose of life, mind, and human striving: to deploy energy and information to fight back the tide of entropy and carve out refuges of beneficial order."

Being in charge is the ability to manage the energy in your physical system the way you want to in order to create the lived experiences you want every day. It's about having the energy to do what you want to do and reducing the energy you use in doing what you don't want to do. It's about countering entropy with negentropy efficiently and effectively, so that the order you want in your system is restored with the least amount of effort on your part.

The best way to start describing what it feels like to be in-charge is to describe what it feels like to not be in-charge, to be in unmitigated disorder. When you feel exhausted, weary, frazzled, insecure, listless, stressed, lethargic, dull, apathetic, bored, disinterested, jaded, or any of the variations of the above, you are not in charge. You are not in charge when you wake up with a sense of dread or ennui about your day, when things you once enjoyed doing feel like chores, when the simplest of tasks feel overwhelming to execute.[1]

Of course, we all feel these things at various points in our lives as a natural part of the human journey, but when we feel like this, more often than not, we are experiencing what the World Health Organization (WHO) calls burnout. Defined as "a syndrome conceptualized as resulting for chronic workplace stress that has not been successfully managed," WHO identifies burnout symptoms as "feelings of energy depletion or exhaustion... negativism or cynicism related to one's job...and reduced professional efficacy."[2] If you think about burnout in the context of efficient energy management, you can see that it isn't about running out of energy to do what you want to do, because the total amount of energy in your physical system does not change.

Burnout is the inefficient—by conscious choice, unconscious default, or external pressure—use of the energy in your system to accomplish the outcomes you want. Burnout is the buildup of entropy without the opportunity and/or action necessary to restore order.

Imagine if you had $100 in $1 bills, and you scattered the $1 bills randomly throughout a large department store. You'd technically still have $100, but every time you wanted to buy something, you would need to run around the store to gather the $1 bills to purchase the thing you wanted. At any point of sale, you'd come up short with what was in your possession; technically, you would have enough but it would just be spread out in a way that made you work too hard to gather the amount necessary to make any purchase. You would also be exhausted after every purchase.

Instead, if you could find a way to keep the 100 $1 bills with you instead of scattering them, you could make the same purchases without the exhaustion.

Burnout isn't about lacking the resources you need; it's about the inefficient scattering of energy so that you consistently don't have enough to do what you want in any given situation.

While WHO has focused primarily on burnout in workplaces, mental health professionals warn us that burnout is as prevalent in our personal lives as it is in our professional lives. Unfortunately for women, we have never had the luxury of seeing the professional and personal as distinctly separate.

As WHO and mental health professionals engaged in in these global conversations about burnout, the COVID pandemic of 2020 ushered in a total collapse of the barriers between our professional lives and personal lives, along with a series of unprecedented stressors that ratcheted our collective burnout to previously inconceivable levels. The events of 2020 taught us that tackling burnout isn't just a professional imperative; it's a personal necessity...especially for women. *Yes, everyone is experiencing burnout at unprecedented levels, but women are experiencing a particularly toxic version of burnout because we were burned the hell out long before 2020.* I was doing a presentation on gender dynamics in the workplace in July 2020 when someone asked me if I was feeling burned out. Before I could formulate a reasoned response to the question, I blurted, "...burned out? I passed burned out in 2015, I think. I'm more charred out than burned out at this point."

It's one thing to have "feelings of energy depletion or exhaustion...negativism or cynicism related to one's job...and reduced professional efficacy," but it's an entirely different story when you have to manage this AND deal with having to cover up who you are, mute yourself to make others feel more comfortable, tone down your anger, smile when you don't feel like smiling, manage the chaos of being the primary caretaker of children and others as the world focuses on something called work-life balance (mythical, as far as I can see), and choose between spending precious time on your appearance or girding yourself against comments about your lack of makeup. And all of the above becomes especially relevant when working with, for, and around men. I believe that we are all working in ways that make us vulnerable to burnout, but women are, more often than not, working in conditions where burnout is the default. It's not a question of *if* burnout will happen, but rather how quickly it will happen after a woman enters the workforce.

This is especially true for working mothers. "Working mothers are much more likely to have experiences of burnout or feeling exhausted, and that's one of the reasons they're considering taking a step back," says Jess Huang, a partner at McKinsey & Company[3].

As one CNBC report summarized, "Juggling childcare challenges with work responsibilities takes a toll. There were about 35 million working mothers in the U.S. at the end of 2019, and roughly 9.8 million of that number are suffering from workplace burnout, according to a new analysis conducted by Great Place to Work and health-care start-up Maven that's based on a survey of 440,000 working parents, including 226,000 mothers." The report also noted that working mothers are 28% more likely to experience burnout than fathers, just because they work and parent, the analysis shows. In the U.S., which means there are 2.35 million additional cases of burnout as a direct result of the home and work demands placed on working mothers. And compared to their White counterparts, Black, Asian, and Latino mothers face higher levels of burnout.[4]

The more I researched burnout, the more "char-out" seems like an actual thing, especially for working moms.

Burnout is the inefficient use of energy. It is the absence of negentropy to counter the effects of entropy in our lives.

In-charge is the opposite of burnout; it is the efficient use of energy. Because you're using energy efficiently, when you're in-charge you feel energetic, rejuvenated, invigorated, excited, active, spirited, animated, strong, refreshed, vivacious, and lively as well as peaceful, balanced, and calm. Being in-charge doesn't mean that you don't have challenging moments or frazzled days or exhausting weeks; it means that feeling challenged and frazzled and exhausted is not your default setting every day. Being in-charge is recalibrating your energy efficiency default to one of positive, invigorated energy, recognizing when you have strayed from that default, and directing your energy back to where you want it to be.

Being in-charge is the deliberate, efficient management of our energy to live the lives we want to live, possessing the ability to direct our energy for optimal achievement however we define that achievement. Whether we are seeking more joy, creativity, peace, endurance, higher levels of success, less vulnerability to burnout, or just greater control of our days and our lives, being in-charge is the path to success that won't destroy you along the way.

And when the rules don't give you much room to manage your energy your way, being in-charge is recognizing that although you don't have the power to change the rules, you always have the power to break them.

When I was in law school, one of my professors asked the class to reflect on this quote by Pablo Picasso: Learn the rules like a pro so you can break them like an artist. She asked us to apply our reflections to the law and told us that following the rules creates stability, but breaking the rules creates change. We had a lively discussion on this topic, and the way she ended that class has always stayed with me. She said that rules maintain the "as is," and the people for whom the "as is" is working will always tell you to follow the rules. And if the "as is" isn't working for you, you can break the rules—or the rules will eventually break you.

Ask yourself if the "as is" is working for you. If it is, follow the rules. If it isn't, you may need to break the rules before the rules break you. Rules help maintain the current reality. Breaking the rules creates new realities. *Being in charge is about deciding for yourself which realities you want to maintain and which ones need to be broken apart to create new realities that work for you.*

YOU, TODAY

Diana

Diana, a working mom, and highly successful sales professional prided herself on being a master juggler of her various responsibilities. She stayed abreast of the latest research on all things related to productivity, time management, and wellness. She was also an early adopter of productivity practices, digital applications, and new ideas—anything and everything—that would help her be more engaged at home, more innovative and productive at work, and a healthier, happier person.

She traveled often for work, and though it was exhausting, she loved what she did, and she was able to manage her travel in a way that worked for her clients and fit into her life the way she wanted it to. A few years ago, she started feeling a shift in her life that she could not explain. She constantly felt tired, not just physically, but mentally and emotionally as well.

One day, Diana was at the airport, waiting at her gate for a flight that was due to board in twenty minutes or so. She decided to check her email one last time before boarding. The next thing she can remember was a flight attendant gently shaking her awake and asking if she was okay. Diana saw that she was still at the airport and asked if the flight was boarding. The flight attendant gently asked her what flight she was trying to board, and Diana replied that she was waiting to board the 6:00 a.m. flight to Washington, DC. The flight attendant told her that it was 3:30 p.m.

Diana didn't initially believe the flight attendant. If that much time had passed, she knew that someone would have called her, and she didn't recall hearing her phone ring at all. She looked down at her phone and saw that she had 32 missed calls.

Diana's life took a dramatic and unexpected turn that day. It wasn't a turn that was visible to others. It wasn't even one that she fully understood that day, but she was on the precipice of changing her life in ways that she could have never imagined. We will come back to Diana's story again through the upcoming chapters. You will also meet other women whose lives embody and illustrate the insights and strategies in this book.

Connect with what resonates in these stories for you. Simply observe what doesn't. Each of us has our own unique, complex, and evolving story, and none of our stories are the same. Yet, the similarities that flowed through the stories of the hundreds of women I interviewed over the past few years are startling. We are all very different, but it seems like we are all, to varying degrees, dealing with the same repetitive shit wreaking havoc in our lives.

Diana Learning

After calling her team to let them know she was okay and apologizing to her vendors profusely, Diana went home and called her doctor. Several weeks of medical appointments, blood tests, and brain and body scans later, Diana had a name for what she had experienced—psychogenic blackout, a stress-induced blackout in which the brain shuts down and doesn't make memories. These blackouts can last a few minutes or several hours, and people can appear to be awake although they aren't actually aware of what's happening around them.

Diana's first reaction to the diagnosis was disbelief. She knew she was exhausted, but she didn't really feel that stressed or anxious. There was nothing in her life that was overly stressful, nothing that she couldn't handle. She took the diagnosis as a sign that she wasn't managing her time well and decided that what she really needed to do was get better at time management and possibly cut back on work a little, especially the travel. She researched coaches and other professionals who could help her fine-tune her time management skills. She was intrigued by the idea of energy management, and we started our work together.

She and I dove into various aspects of her life to discover what was draining her energy, and her answer was a consistent, "There is nothing in my life I necessarily want to change. I know it's all a lot, but it's all stuff I chose, stuff that's important to me." And she would then want to redirect our efforts to find the latest time-management techniques or a new app that could make her more productive so that she could feel energetic again.

The Stress Gap &
Self-Discordant Goals

As I was working with (and worrying about!) Diana, I was also hearing stories from other women about increasing intensity of headaches, depression, chronic pain, sudden onset of autoimmune diseases, insomnia, and just about anything else you can imagine that is a direct derivative of too much negative stress. Women were going to doctors, getting tests, undergoing psychological assessments, and other rigmarole to hear the basic conclusion—they were too stressed out.

In 2018, the *New York Times* published an article entitled "There's a Stress Gap between Men and Women."[5] One of my clients forwarded me the article with her take on the findings; her intro to the article simply read "No shit, Sherlock." Research studies are dramatically consistent in showing how much more stressed-out women are due to more pressure to do housework, childcare, emotional labor at work and at home, and unrealistic standards of how to look and act through it all. Women are far more likely than their male counterparts to engage in "surface acting" at work: as the article says, they express optimism, calm, and empathy even when they are exhausted, pissed off, or feeling anything other than optimistic, calm, or empathetic.[6]

I was happy to see coverage of this issue, but the article's strategies on "how women can push back," were irritatingly—stressfully!—familiar, ridiculous, and unhelpful. The first strategy, "embrace self-care," suggested that women should get more sleep, eat a healthier diet, and exercise more. The second strategy, "know your triggers," was for women to better understand their stressors so that they can apply tailored strategies like... exercise, meditation, and talk therapy. The final strategy, "seek validation"—seriously?????—suggested that "bookstore self-help sections are a good place to start" for validation that your stress is normal and "it is important to talk through these issues [with your spouse or partner] before they come to a head." No shit, Sherlock, indeed.

Yet again, I do not have the vocabulary to fully and accurately express my thoughts and feelings about articles like this. But it is worth reading because it is representative of the kind of drivel that purports to support women but has the opposite effect. It reinforces the idea that women are somehow responsible for their exhaustion because they aren't doing enough—while they are exhausted—to not be exhausted.

So, let's get the basics out of the way, shall we? Self-care is good. Baths are great. Massages are fantastic. We should all sleep more and exercise more. A healthy diet is better than an unhealthy diet, however you are defining it. I can't speak to the self-help section in a bookstore, but bookstores are generally awesome—and many of them have great coffee. It is always important to have conversations with the important people in your life, and it's especially important when the conversations are difficult ones. Therapy is a good thing. Do all these things as much as you want to! But please know that these things don't help us take charge of our lives; they only make us feel slightly better about how shitty it is to not be in charge of the controls of our lives.

We are not stressed out because of what we must do. We are stressed out because of what we must do that we don't want to do.

Being in charge of your life begins with honestly assessing who you really are today and what you actually want today. That assessment has to be free of your guilt for what you didn't get done in the past and your unrealistic expectations of what you think you should do in the future.

This starts with forgiving your past self for what she didn't do and freeing your future self from what you know she doesn't really want to do. Forgive your past self. She did her best with what she knew then. Let her rest. She is not who you are today. Free your future self from everything you think she absolutely has to do. Your future self is still forming; don't get in the way of who you can become by dumping a bunch of shit from the past on her. (I know this is easier said than done, but is it really as complicated as we make it?) This leaves you with your present self—the person who you are today. Who is she really? What does she actually want? Try answering the question fully in the present tense.

To get to the core of who you are and what you want today, it's helpful to quickly review how our brain influences our behavior on a practical level. We have four types of thought processes that act as behavioral triggers: affective (feelings/emotions), cognitive (thoughts/beliefs/knowledge/logic), conative (intention/motivation/volition), and behavioral (choices/actions).[7] All four work together and influence each other, and when they conflict with each other, it causes varying types and levels of stress for us.

Let's say that I want to be healthier by exercising more frequently. My cognitive process—logic—tells me that exercise = health based on what I know about the human body and the world. But my cognitive process will also whisper that while exercise may make me healthier, I'm not exactly unhealthy. So, cognitively, I believe that I will be healthier if I exercise but I also believe that I'm generally healthy in this moment, so maybe I don't really need to prioritize exercising. Maybe I'm okay how I am. Affectively, I may feel good about being the type of person who exercises to be healthy, but I may not like going to the gym or I may not feel like exercise works that well for me or I may not feel like exercising because indulging in a glass of wine or a nap may actually feel better in that moment. Conatively, these different thoughts and feelings make up the motivation I will feel to prioritize this activity, and my behavior will reflect the level of motivation I drum up in my conative process.

If I add something to shift my affective process to be more strongly in favor of exercising, I can influence my conation and eventual behavior. So, I decide that I will exercise with a good friend, and our exercise will be walks where we can catch up and chat. This affective connection with my friend will override the affective value of the wine and the nap, and I will feel better about walking than about wining and napping. My motivation will be stronger, and the probability of me choosing to exercise will be higher. This is the general psychology behind behavioral change, but the story doesn't end there for women.

I have a soft cognitive process for exercising because I know it will be healthy for me, but I think I'm generally healthy. I have a strong affective process because I want to see my friend regularly. This will probably result in a higher conative motivation, and I will be very committed to doing this. It's on my calendar, and I'm ready and able and willing—and then, I get a call from my son that he got hurt at soccer practice. I need to pick him up sooner than I had planned, and I need to cancel the walk with my friend, and I may need to cancel something related to work later as well because I don't know how bad his injury is. Our planned behaviors can be interrupted by a call from a child, a request to turn something around quickly at work, a relative needing a ride somewhere, etc., etc., etc.

A colleague of mine shared an experience that came to her mind as she read a draft of this book:

> As I was reading this, it immediately made me think
> of a story. I have three male cousins who live close to me.

When our grandfather was in his last several years of life and before he had moved into an assisted living facility, he would often fall at home and need someone to come help him get up. I was a single mom taking care of a toddler, managing my mother's medical needs, and working in a fast-paced job. Even though those three male cousins did not need to manage as much as I did, I was the one who got the call every single time. I'd have to ask a colleague to come with me so I could keep up with work, drive across town, and get him situated before returning to continue my 90-hour work week as I did my best to take care of my mother and my child.

High conative motivation usually results in predictable behavior—unless you are the person that gets those calls from work, from children, from relatives, and others. Women get these calls far more than men do in every aspect of their lives, so women's behavior usually doesn't reflect their conation as closely as men's behavior does.

Society's answer to this has been to yell at women to learn how to better set and honor their boundaries. But society is quite hushed when it comes to yelling at the people who violate women's boundaries frequently and consistently.

There are infinitely more resources online for women on how to set boundaries than there are for people on how to respect the boundaries that women set. In my observations and experiences, women don't have problems setting boundaries. We just get exhausted from perpetually having to defend them leading us to eventually decide that it isn't worth the energy expenditure to constantly fight to keep the boundaries in place.

When your affective, cognitive, conative, and behavioral processes are in sync, your energy levels are high, your mood is great, your connection to others is humming beautifully, and you are feeling good! When any one of the processes is out of sync, you experience stress, frustration, and anger, and when more than two of those processes are not in sync, you can experience exhaustion, overwhelm, burnout, and even depression and hopelessness.

Psychologists who study these processes categorize things we want (goals, aspirations, intentions) as either self-concordant or self-discordant.[8] Self-concordant wants are things you actually want; the wants are consistent with what you actually want to do, can do, and feel good doing. Self-concordant wants require that at least three, if not all four, of those processes are in sync. They are rooted in enduring interests and values and have consistency across your feelings, thoughts, motivations, and behaviors.[9]

I have a friend, Sheila, who played basketball in high school and college. She is an incredibly talented player, but what made her so much fun to watch was how much she clearly enjoyed playing. When she was on the court, she was constantly smiling, joking with the other players and the refs, and high-fiving teammates for any and all reasons. She no longer plays competitively, but she doesn't act any differently when she is at the gym playing in a pickup game or practicing by herself. Going to the gym is a self-concordant want for her—she has positive feelings, thoughts, and motivations about playing basketball that drive behavior that reinforces positive feelings, thoughts, and motivations.

Self-discordant wants are those wants that aren't really yours. These are the wants that you have adopted over the years because of familial/social/self pressures, guilt, shame, anger (ooh, those revenge goals are so persistent!), insecurities, and other things that drive you to want to prove something to other people but aren't truly compatible with who you really are. Self-discordant goals usually indicate that two or three out of the four processes are out of sync. Self-discordant goals are more likely than ever before to infect us today because of social media, manipulative advertising, and our collective acceptance of bullshit that isn't real but influences us to create these idealized versions of ourselves that never existed, don't exist today, and will never exist.

I played basketball (not very well) when I was younger, and Sheila has tried to get me to go the gym with her to play basketball. Sometimes she succeeds in getting a commitment from me that I will go to the gym with her. She reminds me that we will get to spend time together and that I really do enjoy playing basketball and the physical exercise will be good for me. I agree with all of it... cognitively. The thought of spending time with Sheila is affectively positive...sort of. I do enjoy spending time with her, but I much prefer a conversation over drinks than being on a basketball court where she kicks my butt every time. I do need the exercise, but I enjoy walking while listening to a podcast or an audiobook much better than I like playing basketball. Committing to go the gym with Sheila is a self-discordant want for me. I mean it so sincerely when I promise her that I will go, but my behavior is heavily influenced by my brain's processes not lining up with going. My idealized self promises Sheila that I will show up; my real self makes the actual decision about whether or not I will go. My idealized self truly believes that my basketball skills will improve dramatically with a little practice; my real self knows better and makes decisions accordingly.

My idealized self is amazing! She is phenomenal at everything she does, she never gets tired, and she never ever looks tired! She reads a lot of books. She would never ever buy a bunch of books with intentions to read them cover to cover and then get frustrated when she doesn't have the time and look up summaries online instead. My idealized self cooks a lot. She never orders out at the last minute because she didn't have the time to cook or because she didn't have the time to go grocery shopping. She meditates every day. She exercises and does yoga every day too. She plans out her days, weeks, and months thoughtfully. She would never ever just do what she needed to get through the day instead of doing exactly what she had planned to do. She sets goals and achieves them. She never procrastinates or surfs the net looking for best practices for writers as a way to actually avoid writing. She never binge-watches Marie Kondo in The Life Changing Magic of Tidying Up on Netflix instead of actually tidying up. And she would never watch videos on how to exercise better as a way to procrastinate exercising. She goes to bed at a reasonable time every night and wakes up ready to do a beautiful morning routine that involves making a fresh smoothie that sets the tone for a beautifully productive day. She would never grab an energy drink instead of making that organic smoothie. She would never let a call from an irritating family member go to voicemail because she just didn't want to deal with the hassle. *My idealized self is amazing in every imaginable way, and this book is not for her because...she does not exist.*

She does not exist, yet most of the goals I have created in the past have been for her. Unfortunately, since she is not real, she has not accomplished most of the goals I've set for her. She's not around to feel the disappointment of not reaching those goals because she is not real, but the disappointment is real, and that real disappointment sticks to the real me. This is the impact of setting self-discordant goals; you will pay a heavy price to achieve them—if you achieve them at all, and the imprint of the price paid, or the disappointment of perceived failure, will stay with you. Most of us respond to this by trying even harder to achieve the self-discordant goals because we want to believe that the disappointment will fade when we achieve the goal.

Achieving self-concordant and self-discordant goals may take the same conative and behavioral efforts, but the efforts toward self-concordant goals leave you with more energy than efforts toward self-discordant goals. For example, two people set the same goal of expanding their professional network. Both cognitively understand that this involves attending events where they can meet and socialize with people they want in their networks. Both have the same conative commitment, and both spend the same amount of time at events. But if one person enjoys meeting new people and networking (positive affection) and the other does not enjoy meeting new people and networking (negative affection), they can both accomplish the goal—but the first person will be energized by the process, and the second person will experience burnout.

My friend Sheila and I can both set the same goal of going to the gym to play basketball. If we both follow through on our goals, Sheila will leave every gym session energized; I will leave exhausted, because it took all my energy to push myself to do this thing that does not yield me enough benefits to be a net positive for my energy.

In many ways, the difference between self-concordant and self-discordant goals isn't whether you will feel good about the eventual outcome, but whether you will feel good about what you have to do to achieve the outcome. *Self-concordant goals are ones where you enjoy the journey to the destination; self-discordant goals are ones where you see the benefit of the destination, but the journey itself exhausts you to the point where you don't reach the destination or are too drained to enjoy the destination upon your arrival.*

Diana Evolving

Diana was focused on learning how to manage her time better so that she could keep going with what she considered a very successful and fulfilling life. She just wanted to live this life without psychogenic blackouts.

When we dug into understanding her affective, cognitive, conative, and behavioral processes, she slowly recognized that while her conative and behavioral processes were in sync (she was excellent at doing what she motivated herself to do), her affective and cognitive processes were not aligned with her conative and behavioral processes. Sure, she was able to will herself to achieve the goals she committed herself to; however, achieving those goals was not making her feel good. She cognitively knew that the goals she was striving for were not matching up with what made her feel good, engaged, and connected to herself and the world around her.

Diana was very good at achieving her goals, but her goals were self-discordant. In order to be successful and feel good (or at least not have stress-induced blackouts), she needed to figure out what she really wanted, what really made her feel good. The more she realized how self-discordant her goals really were, the more she realized that managing her time better but still doing the wrong things would not reduce her stress and exhaustion. She needed to figure out the right things to aspire to. She needed to focus on managing her energy, not her time.

As we discussed this necessary mindset shift that she needed to activate, Diana reflected on how scared she was to make this shift. "I don't know where to start if I have to question the validity of my goals. It's who I am. Who I have always been. I set goals and I achieve them." When I asked her to pinpoint how she decided what goals to set, she told me that she had always reached for the most ambitious goal she could think of in any context. She set a sales quota for herself that was considerably higher than what was considered achievable by the company. She went after clients who were considered moon shots by her colleagues. And she met the ambitious sales quota. She signed a moon-shot client.

Self-discordant goals become especially difficult to give up when you are successful in achieving them, when you are lauded by others as having done something extraordinary.

I asked Diana to consider the possibility that if she had been given a voice in defining what was ambitious that she may have chosen different things. "I was treating goals like they were choices on a menu. I would look at the choices and pick the one that was the hardest, something where I could prove myself," she said.

"What does it mean if I don't select goals off this menu? That's terrifying. You can't just make up what success looks like, can you?"

We are surrounded by menus that present choices for us to select as our goals. But who is in charge of creating these menus? Who is in charge of which choices are—or are not—available on these menus? What if you had the power to create your own menu? What choices would you include as options for goals? Would "get the corner office" or "do more work from home" be on the menu you created? Would "be more authentic" or "be more powerful" make it onto your menu?

I strongly advocate getting more women into positions of authority and leadership because I believe that will change the general choices on menus. But in the meantime, we don't need to limit ourselves to what is listed. Sticking to what's on the current menus maintains the status quo; creating our own menus creates change.

We get to create our own menus, menus that make sense for us because they offer choices that we are excited to select. Hence, the

Great Resignation. And there will surely be those who try to paint the rejection of existing menus as "opting out" or even "failing," but is it possible to opt out of something that we never opted in to?

If you didn't choose to be somewhere, isn't it called escaping when you leave, not opting out?

Even the term "Great Resignation" sugarcoats the tenor of the choices that women are making. When women leave in droves, we politely call it the Great Resignation. In 1981, Johnny Paycheck captured the sentiment women are expressing today perfectly with the lyrics: *You better not try to stand in my way/As I'm a-walking out the door/Take this job and shove it/I ain't working here no more.*

The "Great Take This Job and Shove It" doesn't have the same elegance of the Great Resignation, but the lyrics are damn consistent with what I'm hearing women say as they leave the limited menus of their jobs behind in order to create their own menus.

This is the messy and maybe even terrifying work of being in charge of your life. Being in charge starts with defining what exactly it is that you want to be in charge of; you need to decide which choices you want on your menu. *That process of defining starts with grounding yourself in who you are and what you want today.* It's ensuring that the goals you are working toward are self-concordant in your current reality and rejecting goals that are self-discordant—otherwise known as the shit that is stressing you out!

It will feel like you are just making it up. You will inevitably be asked if you are just making excuses, if you just don't want to work as hard as you possibly can, or if you are just giving up. It can be terrifying to go from achieving in ways that are socially acceptable (even if it's making you stressed, sick, and miserable) to achieving in ways that are acceptable to you.

As you embark on this journey, I want to explicitly state that this book will not create a new menu to replace the existing ones, and it will not give you formulaic bullshit about what you can or should do. This book is a collection of stories, journeys, wisdom, and insights from women just like you and me who have and are challenging the norms and the rules that aren't working for us. This book is about creating your own menu, not about telling you what should be on that menu.

In the next section, we will explore how we create self-concordant goals for who we are and what we want today. Before you continue, take a few seconds to do the following exercise. You can take notes in this book or find some paper to note your observations.

YOU, RIGHT NOW

Inhale deeply through your nose. Exhale forcefully through your mouth. Repeat a couple of times to center yourself.

Then, look around you slowly. Notice where you are. Which city are you in? Is this your home city? Which building are you in? If you are at home, which room are you in?

Notice how you are sitting, what you are wearing, and do a quick scan of your body: start at your toes and move to your calves to your thighs to your hips to your abdomen to your chest to your right arm to your right hand and fingers to your left arm and your left hand and fingers to your neck to your jaw to your eyes and your forehead to your scalp. What did you notice? Is there any pain anywhere? Any aches or tightness? Do the scan in the opposite direction, starting from your scalp and moving back to your toes.

_____

_____

_____

What are some words you would use to describe yourself today? What are some words you would use to describe your profession/career/job/occupation/vocation/daily   activities today? What are some words you would use to describe the people closest to you today? What roles do they play in your life? What are some words you would use to describe where you physically are right now? Is it aesthetically pleasing to you? Is it comfortable?

_____

_____

_____

Now, check in with your emotions. What emotions do you feel right now? Happy? Sad? Excited? Exhausted? Frustrated? Angry? Calm? Anxious? Content? Disgusted? Relaxed? Afraid? Hopeful? Resigned? Anything else?

_____

_____

_____

What are some things you already did today? What are some things you need to do later?

_____

_____

_____

If this moment right now were a color, what color would it be? If this moment had a taste, what would it taste like? If this moment were a song, what song would it be?

_____

_____

_____

Now, take a few more deep breaths, inhaling through your nose and exhaling through your mouth.

This person that you are right now, the person reading this in this moment, the person feeling the things you are feeling right now... this is the person who needs to do the work of defining what you want to do and how you want to be in charge of your life.

Read through your notes. Add anything you want to add. Circle words that really stand out for you. Hold on to this person you are right now as you move to the next section. If you feel yourself losing that sense of being grounded in this moment, review what you wrote.

(You can do this exercise whenever you need to step back from chaos or just get grounded in the present moment.)

THE ELEMENTS OF BEING IN CHARGE

*Peace, Joy, Acknowledgment,
Community...For You Today*

CONNECTING
THE DOTS

Creating self-concordant goals for who you are and what you want today is easy...sort of. A lot has been written about goal setting, but all the research and insights boil down to a simple equation: I want x, and I will do y to achieve x. The goal-setting research dives into the y—how do you start doing y, how do you sustain doing y, who can help you do y, and so on. What all that talk about y ignores is whether the x you are chasing is really the x you want.

This is the crux of being in charge, so let's explore this in more detail.

Goal setting generally goes like this:

1. If you want x, you figure out what the y is to achieve x, and you do y. If you do y to achieve x, and you achieve x, you

will experience the good stuff like pleasure, increase in self-confidence, etc.

2. But, if after doing y, you don't achieve x, you will experience all the bad stuff like negative stress, disappointment, frustration, loss of self-confidence, etc.

If you experience the first scenario, you celebrate. If you experience the second scenario, you try again and again until you achieve the first scenario. If you keep trying, you are demonstrating resilience and determination. If you stop trying, you are demonstrating a defeatist attitude. This is the general logic of goal setting.

What that logic doesn't take into consideration is this: If you do y to get x, and you end up achieving x, *you may still experience all the bad stuff like negative stress, disappointment, frustration, loss of self-confidence, etc. if you never actually wanted x in the first place!*

About ten years ago, I was invited to do a presentation for a group of Fortune 500 CEOs. I prepped for that presentation for hours, and I was ready and confident when I walked into the room. The presentation was received incredibly well; the CEOs asked great questions, and several of them told me that they wanted me to reach out to them as soon as possible so that they could implement some of the ideas within their organizations. After the presentation, the conference planner, who had organized the day and recommended me, excitedly told me how much positive feedback she had already received. I hugged her and thanked her for her trust in me.

She walked me to the elevator, and on the way, she said, "I'd like to give you some unsolicited feedback, if I may." I told her that I would be happy to hear any feedback she had. She cleared her throat a few times and said, "You are really smart. And a really good speaker. You clearly know your stuff." She paused, and I quietly waited for her to continue. What she had just said was clearly not the feedback she was trying to share. She continued, "You really are amazing at what you do, but you just don't look like you take a lot of care with how you put yourself together. You don't look like a professional consultant who commands the fees that you do. You look like...like...a college professor. A cool professor that the kids like, but not a high-profile consultant."

I didn't know how to take her feedback. I asked her what a high-profile consultant looked like, and she told me that I could benefit from working with a personal stylist. I thanked her for the feedback and told her that I wasn't quite sure how to take what she was telling me, but that I would consider it carefully. That evening, I talked to someone I was close to at the time about her comments. He told me that she had a point and that I should consider "upgrading" my look.

I considered this feedback for a few days. I felt like shit. I looked at everything about myself, from my hair to my clothes to my makeup and jewelry, with disdain. Ugh. I had no idea where to start, but I set a goal for myself to hire a stylist and upgrade my look, whatever the hell that meant.

What that meant was that the stylist sent me a 20-page questionnaire on my style (turns out I didn't really have a defined style) and told me that she would come over one day, and we would take everything out of my closet and only put back the items that "deserve to stay." She made me try everything on (I hate—really hate—trying on clothes!) She created "Hell No," "Maybe," and "Hell Yes" piles. Unfortunately, the majority of my clothes went into the Hell No pile based on what she told me was professional. I tried to rescue a few of them, but I could only get them moved into the Maybe pile. I stared at the piles in exhausted resignation as she told me that we would be shopping the next day so that we can acquire items that deserve to be put into my closet. (FYI, I hate—really hate—shopping.)

As I was trying on clothes while shopping, I tried to remind myself that the end result of an upgraded look would be worth this pain. The stylist "curated a wardrobe of essentials" for me, and she took pictures of every item and pictures of how the items went together. She put together an online book for me to refer to if I had questions about what to wear. She also recommended a hair stylist who would "tame" my hair and a makeup specialist who would help me update my cosmetics.

When she left, I put on the worn sweatpants and hoodie I had hidden in the laundry bin and looked at my closet with hopeful skepticism. If I followed the stylist's advice, I should be good. It all felt manufactured and fake to me, but the goal was to upgrade my look, and apparently this was the way to do that.

My upgraded look lasted about four months. I got a lot of compliments on my outfits and my hair, but everyone who really knew me asked if I was okay. When I looked in the mirror, I could tell that I looked more polished, but I didn't look like me. I found myself worrying about how I appeared on stage instead of what I was going to say. I got exhausted in the morning just thinking about putting an outfit together. I had achieved the upgrade, but I was miserable, and during my presentations my energy levels were compromised, reflecting the energy drain of maintaining this upgraded version of myself every single day.

One day, in the middle of a particularly long presentation, a client asked me if I was feeling okay. She said that I didn't look that great, and if I wasn't feeling well, we should reschedule the remainder of the presentation. I told her I was fine. She didn't believe me and reiterated that we should reschedule. I realized that she was not asking me if I wanted to reschedule. She was telling me to reschedule because I was not doing my job well that day.

That night, ensconced comfortably in my sweats, I reflected on the irony of what had happened. I had upgraded my look, but at the cost of downgrading my work. I was spending so much time looking the part of a high-profile consultant that I had compromised the work that had made me a high-profile consultant.

I love what I do. I love the work of researching, writing, and teaching the complex concepts that help us live and work better. I don't love worrying or even thinking about my outfits or hair or makeup. I had to literally and metaphorically erase my goal of changing my look. There is nothing left in my closet from my upgrade attempt. I now follow Steve Jobs' sage style guidance of wearing a uniform so that you don't have to waste time choosing what to wear. Everything in my closet is black now; everything matches everything. It's easy for me to pick out what to wear every morning (it doesn't really matter because everything looks mostly the same), and it's easy for me to shop online for anything I need to replace. I've stopped trying to wrestle my hair into a style and work with what it wants to do that day.

Writing a book is a self-concordant goal for me. I enjoy the tough work of researching, conceptualizing, writing, and editing. It's hard, but the challenges energize me to dig deeper and do better. Worrying about my wardrobe and style is a self-discordant goal for me. The challenges deflate and drain me.

Achieving goals that aren't truly our goals feels very similar to not achieving goals. Success at what you don't really want can often feel the same as failure. We badass women know how to achieve the goals we really want to achieve. We know how to do the y to get to x. We don't need books on motivation and ambition and all that crap. We just need to take a good hard look at what our goals are and be unflinchingly honest with ourselves if the x we are chasing is the x we really want.

How do we know if x is what we really want? We look at y (what you have to do to achieve x) and ask ourselves if y brings us **peace, joy, acknowledgment, and community**; if y brings us these things, x is what we really want. If y doesn't bring us these things, achieving x will never make us feel in charge.

This is the underbelly of goal setting that people don't like to talk about. Achieving goals only makes us happy if what we have to do to achieve the goals brings us peace, joy, acknowledgment, and community. This is especially true for women because most of the choices available on socially acceptable menus of goals were created by men for whom the pursuit of those goals was possible, enjoyable, and sustainable.

The more I observed my clients, my friends, and myself experience consistently high levels of negative stress, disappointment, and frustration, even as we achieved the ambitious goals we set for ourselves, the more I realized that we weren't chasing the right goals. After dozens of interviews with psychologists, philosophers, and other experts on the human experience, as well as hours of research on stress and happiness, I had a breakthrough insight that changed my approach to my work in this area.

You can be successful and confident and excited about your life *and* be stressed to the point of physical, emotional, and mental collapse at the same time. *Achieving self-discordant goals will land you in this convergence of success and stress, a place where many successful women find themselves. It's a place where nothing is wrong—but nothing feels good, either.*

Stress is medically defined as your response to negative physical, mental, or emotional pressures that cause chemical changes in your body that lead to all the bad things we want to avoid, like high blood pressure, accelerated heart rate, frustration, anxiety, depression, etc. Stress can be a good thing, because we need those chemical changes to deal with negative experiences. But when the negative experiences become too frequent or inescapable, stress becomes chronic; it becomes a condition we live with constantly instead of a temporary response to a situation. This type of stress makes you sick and leads to burnout. It is not the absence of happiness, success, confidence, and other positive emotions; it's also not about doing too much or not getting enough sleep. This type of stress is a direct result of not feeling like you are in charge of your own life.

Imagine that you decided to drive from Manhattan to Los Angeles. There are a multitude of decisions you would need to make to embark on this journey. What kind of car will you drive? Will you drive by yourself, or will you have someone in the car with you? Who will you invite? What route will you take? How long do you want this journey to take? Are there places along the way that you really want to stop and explore? Are there people along the way that you want to visit? Will you stay in hotels, camp, or crash with friends along the way? Will you listen to podcasts or music or audiobooks? How will you choose what you listen to? What will you wear during this drive?

Assume getting to Los Angeles makes you happy. You are excited about what awaits you in Los Angeles. You are confident in your ability to make this trip. This has been an ambition of yours for a long time. You are prepared. You are ready to get on the road and start driving. Savor that feeling for a second.

Now, imagine that although you really want to invite one person, you feel the pressure or are told to invite someone else. Imagine that you are told what kind of car to drive, the route to take, the stops you will make, how long it will take you to make the trip, what you will listen to in the car, and even what you should wear during the drive. Imagine if the rationale behind these decisions was professionalism or tradition or because that's the way it's always been done.

You really are excited about making this trip. You really are excited to get to Los Angeles. You tell yourself that you can put up with the details of the actual drive, but with each passing hour of not stopping where you want to stop, not listening to what you want to listen to, not being comfortable in what you have on, engaging in conversations you aren't interested in, etc., the drive starts feeling unbearable.

I use this road trip metaphor in my coaching sessions to help women see the difference between negative stress and reasonable exhaustion. It is reasonable on a road trip to be exhausted after driving for six or seven hours in a day. It is reasonable for your body to ache because you were crunched in a seated position all day. It is even reasonable for your mind to be tired after navigating the road for a day. But it is not reasonable for your body to be in pain because you couldn't stop when you wanted to. It is not reasonable for a pounding headache to take root because you had to listen to someone else's music, especially if it was music that you really didn't like. It is not reasonable for your blood pressure to be increased because none of the places you wanted to stop were sanctioned as legitimate stops.

You still want to go to Los Angeles. You still like road trips. You are still a great driver. But you are starting to really dislike this particular trip with this particular companion and this particular navigation strategy. That dislike—often coated with a healthy dose of anger and resentment—is what burns women out. The destination rocks, but the ride sucks.

Loving the destination but hating the ride is why so many women reported feeling more productive and connected to their work when they weren't going into the office every day during the pandemic. It's why so many women are demanding that their workplaces don't return to their pre-pandemic format. It's why we are in the middle of a "Great Take This Job and Shove It" movement by women.

Joni is a senior partner at a law firm who works primarily with investment banks, private equity funds, and hedge funds. She had been perpetually stressed out for years, and she had internalized the narrative that her job was just a stressful one. She was initially frustrated at the start of the pandemic when all of her in-person meetings with clients became virtual. But within a couple of months, she realized that she was doing more work than she had ever done before—but she was less stressed. She was enjoying her work more because she didn't have to deal with the social dynamics of lunches and happy hours as precursors to getting the work done. "I don't miss the frat-boy preamble to the substantive work conversations. I have more energy to do the work, and I forgot how much I really enjoy the work. I dread the return to that shit. I want the pandemic to be over, of course. But I have found myself hoping that the way we are working continues for long enough that it becomes our new normal."

Better understanding the stress of the sucky ride helped me see what women were really saying in my interviews and coaching sessions. No matter the x that women were pursuing, the y necessary to get the x was causing stress unless the y itself led to peace, joy, acknowledgment, and community. And, if the y led to peace, joy, acknowledgment, and community, the chronic stress wasn't triggered whether x was achieved or not. This is not to suggest that peace, joy, acknowledgment, and community led to a problem-free utopian experience; they just reduce the relentless chronic stress that makes us sick so that we can experience the normal ups and downs of being human.

Why peace, joy, acknowledgment, and community? Why not financial freedom or better relationships or a better job or a promotion or a better home or a bigger retirement fund or more travel or entrepreneurial ventures or romance or the myriad of other things that usually fill up our New Year's resolutions and bucket lists? All of these were, of course, on the table, but when I dug deeper into the why behind those things, the resoundingly consistent themes I heard in the replies were peace, joy, acknowledgment, and community. Why financial freedom? Because financial freedom was the key to peace. Why more travel? Because travel and new experiences led to joy. Why a promotion? Because a promotion led to acknowledgment. Why better relationships? Because better relationships led to community.

In my interviews and coaching sessions, I played around with different versions of these concepts. For example, was joy the same as happiness? Was peace the same as contentment? Was community the same as family? Was acknowledgment the same as recognition? And countless hours of linguistic philosophizing later, the words that resonated the most concisely and clearly for women were peace, joy, acknowledgment, and community.

If different words resonate for you, please use those words. The following strategies will still hold insights that are useful for you, even if you prefer contentment over peace or happiness over joy or anything else. I do recommend that you identify four values that connect deeply with you if peace, joy, acknowledgment, and/or community don't resonate with you.

This idea of "it's the journey, not the destination" has been affirmed in various cultures throughout history, and that message—as clichéd as it is—seems to be the unifying theme in the stories that women shared with me. And, regardless of the destination, the journey that resonated most positively for women is a journey filled with peace, joy, acknowledgment, and community, in that order.

Start with peace.

Then, add joy.

Then, sprinkle in some acknowledgment.

Then, connect with your community to pull everything together.

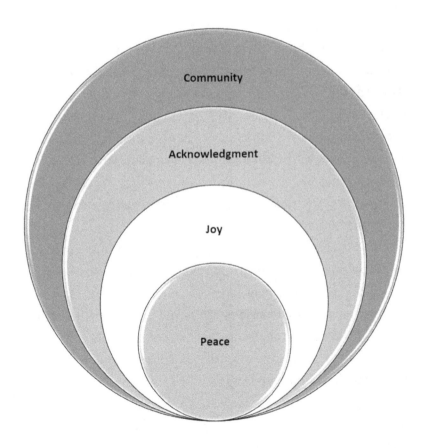

Defining Peace...For You Today

There are two types of "tired," I suppose.
One is a dire need of sleep, the other is a dire need of peace.
—Mandeq Ahmed

Peace of mind for five minutes,
that's what I crave.
—Alanis Morissette

Unlike joy, acknowledgment, and community, which reflect the presence of things we want, *peace is the absence of things we don't want*. Peace is defined as freedom from disturbance, internal or external. We may have different definitions of disturbance in our lives, but our definition of peace is beautifully similar: ***Peace is the absence of the bullshit draining your energy.*** That bullshit can be circumstances, people, or just stuff; it can be temporary or it may have lasted longer than you intended. It's the stuff that makes your shoulders tense, your head hurt, your back ache, your jaw clench, your stomach roil, your skin heat, and your fists clench. Yes, our bodies are amazing at signaling disturbances for us, and they are equally amazing at signaling peace.

Peace is indeed the absence of disturbance, but more precisely, it's the absence of disturbance that you didn't choose. As we pursue peace, joy, acknowledgment, and community, we will choose to take on endeavors that cause us stress and exhaustion, but stress and exhaustion of our choosing does not feel like a disturbance in the same way as stress and exhaustion that is forced upon us. Stress and exhaustion of our choosing feels like the hard work necessary for living our lives the way we want to. Stress and exhaustion of our choosing make our bodies tired, but they don't make our bodies hurt in the way a lack of peace does.

Peace, in the context of being in charge of our own lives, is not the absence of stress or exhaustion. Peace is the absence of stress and exhaustion that we did not choose and would never choose for ourselves if we had the choice. Almost every single woman I interviewed for this project and have coached in this area talked about peace as the primary objective in their lives. Peace.

Britt

Britt is one of those women that seems to have lived many lifetimes in this current life. She had been a physician for many years. She invented a biomedical device, patented it, and sold the patent to a company. She adopted two children who are now thriving adults. Oh, and she travels the globe running marathons, "seeing the world 26.2 miles at a time."

During our first interview, Britt exuded confidence and grace. She was open and honest about her life and shared lots of insights about how she achieved all that she had in her life. As we started winding down the interview, I asked her to describe a few moments in her life when she had experienced a sense of peace. Britt asked if she could have a few minutes before she continued. She came back on the line after about five minutes and asked me if it would be okay for us to continue the interview at another time because I had given her a lot to think about and she wanted to reflect on this idea of peace before she answered me.

I was surprised by her request and curious as to what had triggered her mood shift during the interview.

We spoke again a few days later, and I started our conversation by asking her to share what she had reflected on since our first conversation. She told me that she had been really excited throughout the conversation to share how she had followed her passions and how she had achieved her goals. But she said that my question about what gave her peace in her life had given her pause. "I'm not sure I have peace in my life. I push to do stuff. I get things done. I go places. But I don't know if I have peace in my life. My daughter has told me that I run marathons so that I never have to stand still. She said I was scared of standing still and catching up to myself."

She talked at length of feeling like she always needed to be moving forward, achieving more. She wasn't sure when it had started or why, but she realized that while she was proud of everything she had accomplished, she wasn't sure she had really enjoyed the moments that added up to the successes.

With each subsequent conversation, she dug a little deeper. I asked her to do an exercise in which she listed all the successes in her life. I told her to list at least twenty-five. That was not a problem for her. She had more than fifty within ten minutes. I then asked her to take a deep breath and look at each success and ask herself if she would have pushed to achieve that success if she had to keep the achievement a secret. How many of these successes would have still felt good if she couldn't tell anyone about them?

This exercise, designed to separate intrinsic motivation from extrinsic motivation, took her much longer than listing her successes. When she was done, she was in tears. She only had three things on the list that she would have done even if no one ever knew about them…adopting her children, running marathons, and volunteering at her community medical clinic. As she studied her list, she told me that she felt peace when she did these three things. She was doing them for the purpose of doing them, not just to get them done.

Extrinsic motivators are not always bad (we'll get to their good qualities when we talk about acknowledgment), but they don't lead to peace. Peace is the absence of stress and exhaustion that isn't intrinsically chosen by you. And, without peace, you cannot enjoy what you are doing; you cannot enjoy the journey, and even when you reach the destination you are striving for, the pleasure of achievement is short-lived.

You, Peaceful

Inhale deeply through your nose. Exhale forcefully through your mouth. Repeat a couple of times to center yourself.

Take a piece of paper and divide the page into three columns. Label the columns "What I Do/Did," "What I Get/Got," and "Yes/No."

In the first column, start writing your achievements, successful habits, positive things you do, etc. These are things you are proud of doing/having done. After you make a list (try and list at least twenty-five things in this column), move to the second column.

In the second column, write down two or three words next to each success/achievement that describe what you get from doing/having done that thing. Don't overthink it. Don't censor yourself. Don't edit it. See what words flow out of you naturally.

After you finish the second column, take a few minutes to look over your lists. What patterns are you seeing? What is surprising to you? What resonates with you? Reflect on these questions for a few minutes before moving onto the third column.

In the third column, think about whether what you wrote in the second column would still be true if the item in the first column was accomplished in secrecy.

If no one ever knew about it, would you still get the benefits you listed in the second column? If you would get the same benefits if this were accomplished in total secrecy, write "yes," and if the benefits would evaporate or change dramatically if external eyes couldn't view it, write "no."

Circle the items in the first column that have a "yes" marked in their corresponding row in the third column. What do you notice about what you have circled? Are there any commonalities shared by the things you have circled?

Keep this list somewhere where you can glance at it from time to time. It's a quick reminder of what in your life is fueled by extrinsic motivators and what is fueled by intrinsic motivators.

What I Do/Did	What I Get/Got	Yes/No

As we transition from peace to joy, remember that peace is the foundation to being in charge of your life. It's not possible to feel in charge if you aren't experiencing peace, and peace isn't the absence of stress...it's the absence of stress you did not choose and would not choose if you had been given the choice.

Defining Joy...For You Today

We hold these truths to be self-evident,
that all men are created equal,
that they are endowed by their Creator
with certain unalienable rights,
that among these are Life, Liberty,
and the pursuit of Happiness.
— The Declaration of Independence of the
United States of America

Putting aside the "all men are created equal part," the rights to liberty and the pursuit of happiness are very interesting wants to express. We often use the terms *liberty* and *freedom* interchangeably, but the difference between the two is critical to women as we seek a better understanding of how to be in charge of our lives. There are a lot of philosophical discussions on this difference, but the general distinction is that freedom is the power to choose what you want to say and do, and liberty is the power to actually say and do what you want to say and do. Liberty is a form of freedom, but not all freedoms are liberties.

For example, if I'm asked to share a secret that I have been told not to share, I have the freedom to share it, but I don't have the liberty to do so because I need permission from the person who told me the secret. I have the freedom to drive as fast as I want to, but the law restricts my liberty to do so without negative consequences. Freedom is the state of being able to do something. Liberty is the power to do what you want without negative consequences as constructed by social norms, laws, etc.

Women have the freedom to do a lot of things that we don't have the liberty to do. When we fight to change the laws, policies, biases, and various other things that negatively impact women's lives, we are, more often than not, fighting for the liberty to say and do things that we have the freedom to say and do without negative consequences. The difference between freedom and liberty for women in our world today seems to be the difference between what we can/want to do and what we have social permission to do as enforced by negative consequences if not heeded. To be in charge of our own lives in today's world means understanding that gap between our freedoms and our liberties.

I'm not suggesting that the consequences of doing something you don't have the liberty to do aren't substantial or difficult to endure. Better understanding the gap between your freedoms and your liberties allows you to make more conscious choices about exactly what you want and don't want in your life.

The "pursuit of happiness" listed as an unalienable right on the heels of liberty in the Declaration of Independence is just as interesting as the choice of liberty, because the phrase implies happiness is a prize we win after we pursue it. We all have a right to the chase, but do we all have the same rights to the prize at the end of the chase? The "pursuit of happiness" tells us nothing about actually being happy. This raises several issues that impact our ability to take charge of our own lives. At the risk of philosophizing this issue beyond practical application: *Even though we are told we have the right to pursue happiness, do we have the liberty*

to do so if our definition of happiness doesn't fit with the social norms?

If being an active and engaged mother in my children's lives makes me happy, do I have the liberty to pursue that happiness in today's workplaces that define success in a way that demands too much of my time? If dressing in comfortable leggings and tunics makes me happy, do I have the liberty to pursue that happiness in the same way as someone who is happy wearing a suit? If the answer is a no to either of those questions, who created those rules? Who voted to make them norms? Who enforces those rules? How unalienable is this right to pursue happiness if you don't have a meaningful say in deciding what makes you happy?

This inquiry into liberty and happiness helps us understand that if the rules aren't made by us and for us, exercising our freedoms will often mean breaking the rules. But that's not as scary as it sounds, because most women arrive at this juncture, break the rules, and discover that the negative consequences were empty threats that didn't materialize as we were told they would.

Alicia Keys no longer wearing makeup...with positive feedback from her fans. Tammy Duckworth breastfeeding her baby on the U.S. Senate floor...and the rules being changed to allow infants on the Senate floor. Beyoncé performing on a global stage in the ninth month of her pregnancy...to some of the highest ratings ever recorded for a live performance. A trans woman running for office in North Carolina...and winning. A Black and Indian woman presidential candidate roundly criticizing another presidential candidate...and being selected by him to become the first female, first South Asian, and first Black person to become Vice President of the United States.

These are just the stories covered by the media. There are countless other stories of women breaking rules and creating liberties for themselves and for all women that did not exist before. Liberty and the pursuit of happiness may be articulated as unalienable rights in the U.S. Declaration of Independence, but being in charge of our lives as women often involves taking liberties with the rules to pursue something that is far more accessible and powerful than happiness—joy.

> *When we focus on joy, happiness finds us.*
> *Happiness is a broad evaluation of how we feel about our*
> *lives...often measured over time.*
> *Joy is much simpler and more immediate.*
> *—Ingrid Fetell Lee*

Happiness is an outcome; joy is our enthusiasm about the actions that lead to the outcome. We often treat the differences between these two words as merely semantic, but the research on energy management clearly demonstrates that the difference is quite significant. We often tend to define happiness based on extrinsically motivated goals—how much money we make, what kind of house we live in, what our job titles tell us about our career progression, which schools we or our children attend, what kind of clothes, shoes, jewelry, we wear, etc. Joy, on the other hand, is what we feel in each present moment in each day. It is how excited we are to interact with the people we are connected to, the pleasure of a warm cup of tea on a cold and rainy day, the anticipation of jumping into that work assignment, the unplanned unhurried time with family and friends, etc.

We have relegated joy to the realm of rest and relaxation, but it is very difficult to be in charge of our lives if we are not experiencing joy in the activities that lead to the goals we have set, and if we aren't experiencing joy in the pursuit of happiness to which we are told we have an unalienable right. Joy in the journey to the goal is what makes a goal a self-concordant goal.

If women were involved in the writing of the U.S. Constitution, I do believe that our inalienable rights would have been written very differently.

The Schuyler Sisters
Hamilton the Musical

[Angelica, Eliza & Peggy Schuyler]
"We hold these truths to be self-evident
That all men are created equal"

[Angelica Schuyler]
And when I meet Thomas Jefferson (unh!)
I'mma compel him to include women in the sequel.

Harper

Harper contacted me because she was frustrated about not being able to meet the long list of goals she had set for herself. She told me that she had always been able to set a lot of goals and push herself to meet them. "I wonder if something is wrong with me. I can't push myself like I used to."

At the beginning of our work together, she had seventeen goals she wanted to achieve in the next year. (You read that right! Seventeen!) She is a successful entrepreneur whose ten-year-old company was valued at around five million dollars. She had a great team, and she loved her work. "I started my company in a closet, and I would still do this out of a closet if I needed to," was something she said often to her team and to her clients. The joy she felt in doing her work every day was clearly evident.

We began by doing the intrinsic-extrinsic motivators exercise, and she whittled her list from seventeen to eight. I asked her to take the eight remaining goals and imagine that she had one hour a day that she had to dedicate to each goal. I asked her to list three things she would do in that hour for each goal. We brainstormed together to get that list of twenty-four activities, and I asked her to rate each activity on a scale from zero to ten, with zero being nothing short of torture to engage in this activity and ten being blissful even when challenging.

When she completed the ratings, I asked her to cross out all the goals where none of the activities rated above a five. She protested at crossing out the goals. "But I really want these goals!" she said. But even as she acknowledged the ones that needed to be crossed out, but she resisted actually crossing them out. I asked her to write the goals that remained on a separate piece of paper. Her list of eight was now halved, to four. We were finally getting somewhere, even as she frequently gazed longingly at the longer list.

Harper's next assignment was to add up the ratings numbers for each goal and list the four in descending order. The goal at the very top was to plan and take a vacation to Croatia, specifically the small town where her mom had been born and raised. The second goal was to plan and do more girls' nights with her two best friends. The third goal was to stop outsourcing her gardening and plant and nurture her garden herself. The fourth goal was to create a strategic charitable giving strategy for her company and for herself so that she could make a bigger impact for the causes she cared about.

When Harper looked at these goals, she told me that the exercise had not worked. "These aren't the real goals," she insisted. "These are just things I want to do." I reminded her that she had put them on her original list of seventeen goals, so she must have seen them as goals at some point. "Okay, they are goals, but they are not real goals. Real goals are harder to do, right?"

I asked her to tell me one of the "real goals" that had made the first cut from seventeen to eight, but hadn't made the cut from eight to four. "I want to write a book about my experiences as an entrepreneur," she said. "I know it will be helpful to a lot of women. It's based on questions I get asked all the time." We looked at the activities she had listed for that goal: write, edit, rewrite. Each of the activities was rated as a four. When I asked her to tell me about the ratings, she told me that she hated writing. She hated editing and rewriting even more.

When I probed her as to why she had this goal of writing a book if she hated writing so much, she said she really wanted the lessons she'd learned to be available to female entrepreneurs. "Is it more important to you that the book exists or that you write the book?" I asked. "That the book exists…oh shit, I get it. I need a ghost writer." She rewrote the goal from writing a book to getting her insights published and realized that many of the initial tasks were something she could delegate.

The saying "life is a journey, not a destination," is not quite accurate. Life is a series of destinations each with multiple winding journeys, but enjoying the journeys as you travel them is what makes those destinations worth pursuing.

After peace, joy was the want that most women expressed as necessary to feeling present and engaged in their lives, but their definitions of joy were not idealized concepts of not having any problems or trying to feel good all the time. They were about the act of being in a state of joy. As Mark Manson so poetically notes in *The Subtle Art of Not Giving a F*ck*, "No matter where you go, there's a five-hundred-pound load of shit waiting for you. And that is perfectly fine. The point is not to get away from the shit. The point is to find the shit you enjoy dealing with."

Joy is not about avoiding shit; it's about choosing the shit you want to deal with because, yeah, you enjoy it. When I was working with Harper, she asked me if I enjoyed writing. I lit up and told her that I loved writing, from conceptualizing an idea to organizing a flow of ideas to playing with vocabulary to editing to sharpen the message. She just stared at me as if what I was saying was so foreign to her that she could not comprehend what the words meant. I asked her if she enjoyed experimenting with fitness protocols and motivating people to work out. She lit up and started talking about workout equipment and isolating muscle groups and something else and something else. She looked as excited when she was talking about fitness as she looked worn out when she was talking about writing.

That is the beauty of joy. We all find joy in different things, and if each of us concentrated our efforts on what brings us joy, we would not only be in charge of our lives (lit up from the inside out), but we would arrive at our chosen destinations juiced up and ready to keep going instead of depleted and worn out.

✳ Diana Letting Go ✳

As Diana and I were working through the exercises of what she really wanted today, what motivated her intrinsically, and how she defined peace and joy, she became overwhelmed and asked if we could take a break from our work. I did not hear from her for a couple of months. When she restarted our sessions, she told me what had overwhelmed her was our work on peace and joy. It had demonstrated to her that her greatest drain of peace and joy was her marriage to an emotionally and physically abusive husband.

"I wasn't scared of leaving him for financial reasons or at the prospect of being a single mother. I was scared of failing at my marriage, failing at something that was probably killing me as I tried to save it." Her voice shook as told me that she had been in the middle of getting yelled at by her husband when she saw that there was no peace or joy to be salvaged or gained in the relationship.

"I had always believed that if I tried hard enough, I would have a happy marriage. I realized that I had no idea if my marriage would ever be a happy one, but it was not going to lead me to peace or joy anytime soon. As he was yelling at me, I saw how wild his eyes were, how he was sneering, how much it looked like he wanted to and would have enjoyed hurting me, and I asked him to leave. It came out of nowhere. He looked more surprised than I felt, and I repeated my request for him to leave. He left. I had no idea how this would work or what the future would look like, but in that moment, I felt peace. As upset as I was, I slept more soundly that night than I had in a very long time."

She told me that she was seeing a therapist and a lawyer, and she was ready to figure out how to better manage her energy now that her biggest energy drain was not in her space every day.

I sent her a copy of *The Subtle Art of Not Giving a F*ck* by Mark Manson and told her that we could go as slow as she wanted. She laughed and said that while she had been slow to ask him to leave, she did not want to take it slow in taking charge of her life.

Diana's story, unfortunately, was not the first or the last one I heard that involved a separation or divorce. Working on energy management involves leading women to address issues in their personal lives that they need to confront honestly, to make the tough decisions that might initially cause more chaos yet offer the only perceptible path to peace and joy. While most of my coaching clients initially contact me because they want to manage/fix/improve something in their professional lives, what happens in women's professional lives cannot be easily segregated from what happens in their personal lives. And even when women think they can separate the professional and the personal, the world will not let them.

When I reflect on what my doctor told me when I had pneumonia, I know that one of the things that irritated me the most about his "advice" was that he did not ask me to consider all aspects of my life and make necessary changes for wellness; he only recommended that I quit working. People—both men and women—blur the line between professional and personal for women so much that it does not make sense for women to treat the two realms differently. Managing your time better at work can lead to filing for divorce, and making peace with conflicts at home can lead to better energy management at work.

When we reach for more peace and joy in our lives, we will find ourselves fusing our professional and personal lives, because *we were not the ones that separated them.* Some people find it easier to compartmentalize than others, but the truth is, the two realms were never separate for women. They became separate only to make gendered roles work. Treating the personal and professional as two separate parts of our lives reminds me of the time when restaurants and planes had separate smoking sections right next to the "non-smoking" area. As a child, I used to watch the smoke drift persistently into the non-smoking section of the restaurant and wonder how this setup possibly made sense. I wondered what adults had figured out that I had not, because I just couldn't see how you could command the smoke to stay in one place.

The truth was that adults had not figured it out. They had just created a fake solution to a real problem so that they could feel like they were doing something while actually doing nothing.

I have often felt like separating my professional and personal lives followed the logic of having a smoking section in restaurants. You can isolate things in theory, but life, like smoke, would persistently occupy all the separated spaces without differentiation.

Integrating these artificially separated parts is a natural outcome of taking charge of our lives. Peace and joy cannot exist in a life that is sliced up into theoretical pieces that don't make sense in any actual woman's life.

Louise and Esme
The Different Faces of Peace & Joy

＊Louise and Her "Bob Problem"＊

Louise was a senior manager in a manufacturing company when she and I started working together. She had been attending an executive MBA program in the evenings. When she was about six months away from completing the program, she reached out to me to help her plan her next career moves. Her supervisor had told her that she would be promoted to a director position as soon as she received her MBA, and Louise wanted to make sure that she negotiated the promotion, the transition, and the ensuing new role successfully.

We talked about what she really wanted in her life, and we started creating an action plan for her to execute. One of Louise's biggest challenges as she prepared to leave her current role and transition to a new one was her high stress level due to her volume of work, balancing work and classes, and anxiety about her ability to prove herself in the new role. Her stress had taken a toll on her health, and she told me that she had been taking medications for high blood pressure and anxiety management for several months.

When we started exploring how she was defining and experiencing peace in her life, she told me that she felt that her current life was not very peaceful, but she believed that she would "find peace" once she was settled into her new position. We talked through the difference between "finding peace" and "creating peace," and the importance of her creating peace for who she was in that moment.

I asked Louise to keep a peace log for a week. She was to pause a few times a day to note her peace level from one to ten, with one being **"STRESS I DID NOT CHOOSE"** and ten being **"STRESS I WOULD CHOOSE."** I asked her to note a few words after her peace number to capture what she felt was causing that number to be what it was. I mentioned to Louise that it could be as informal as she wanted, and she could use her phone or a small memo pad. Louise decided to make it a formal process for herself. She committed to checking in four times a day with herself at 7:00 a.m., 12:00 p.m., 5:00 p.m., and 10:00 p.m., for seven days. She used a journal that her sister had given her for her birthday.

When we met to go over her log, I was surprised by how closely she had stuck to the process she had outlined. She had checked in four times a day, just as she had planned. She had also created three columns on each page of the journal: Time of Day, Peace Level, and Notes. I asked her how she felt organizing and writing in this journal, and she beamed. "I loved thinking through how I would organize it and write in it so that I can see things quickly. Some of the most peaceful parts of my day were opening the journal, seeing the columns, and making my notes." Her smile was radiant...and in stark contrast to how her face looked when she talked about the content of the log.

Over the week that Louise had kept this log, the highest peace level she had logged was a five, and she had only logged a five twice. Almost all the levels she had logged were threes and fours, with a few ones and twos sprinkled in as well. She asked me if it was unusual for someone to have such low peace levels, and I candidly shared with her that women's peace levels tended to be quite low unless they were deliberately creating, monitoring, and managing the causes of stress in their lives. We talked about the concept of peace as "stress you didn't choose," a definition that allows women to differentiate between stress that energizes and stress that drains. Louise reflected on this and noted that she liked the stress of studying and writing papers for her MBA program. She also liked the stress of doing home improvement projects in her house and planning get-togethers with family and friends. She liked the stress of setting goals and pushing herself to achieve them. She liked the stress of digesting the large amounts of information she needed to at work in order to create the insights that helped people make better operating decisions.

It was clear that Louise thrived on structure, hard work, and pushing herself to grow. So, why were her peace levels so low? As we dug into her notes, I reminded her that she had attributed her high levels of stress to "volume of work, balancing work and classes, and anxiety about her ability to prove herself in the new role" and asked her to look for any consistent causes of her lack of peace, especially as they related to her perception of her primary stressors. She read over her notes a few times and suddenly exclaimed, "Oh my god! I do not have a stress problem. I have a Bob problem!"

Bob was Louise's supervisor. Louise's journal revealed that almost every note mentioned Bob. "Bob dumped last-minute stuff on me. I'm going to have to stay up late to finish work and get my paper done." "I was late for class because Bob messed up the time for the call. I hate being late." "Had my one-on-one with Bob today, and he wasn't giving me a straight answer on my promotion." "I can't get a read on what Bob thinks I need to show to lock down the promotion." "Bob clearly hasn't read the reports."

As soon as Louise named her lack of peace as a "Bob problem," she started laughing...and she could not stop laughing for several minutes. Every time she tried to stop laughing, she would only end up laughing harder. Tears were running down her face, and she was trying to catch her breath between fits of laughter. When she could finally speak again, she said, "I have a Bob problem!" and burst into laughter again.

It was impossible to not laugh along with her, and we spent most of our time together that day laughing. When Louise's laughter had trickled down to intermittent giggles, she apologized to me for "wasting" our session. I told her that she had probably released more stress through her laughter than she would have through any strategies we would have brainstormed, and she had defined the source of her lack of peace more succinctly than I had ever seen it done. Now that she knew she had a "Bob problem," the next step was to figure out what to do to neutralize it.

Louise realized that she really liked her work, but her untenable volume of work was caused by Bob dumping his work on her. She loved school, but was having trouble balancing work and school because Bob was not respecting her schedule. She was excited about a promotion and knew that she could handle the new responsibilities that came with it, but she was constantly anxious because Bob's promise of the promotion wasn't lining up with his actions of making that promotion happen. Louise had joy in her life—she loved what she had created in her life—but she could not access that joy because of the lack of peace.

Once Louise had pinpointed the cause of her lack of peace, she asked Bob if they could meet to talk about her promotion. Bob rescheduled their meeting twice and told her he did not have time to meet with her about that until after she had received her MBA. She reminded him that the promotion would be triggered when she matriculated and that she would feel better if they proactively planned for the transition. He never responded.

Louise went to HR and discovered that Bob had never noted anything about a promotion for her, nor had he budgeted for it. The HR representative she worked with confidentially told Louise that Bob had a reputation in the company for finding good workers and keeping them under him to make himself look good. Louise dug a little deeper into her department's hiring and promotion numbers and realized that Bob had only hired women in this role, and none of the women had ever been promoted. They had all quit. The "Bob problem" was a bigger problem than she had realized.

I had expected Louise to feel dejected or even more stressed out after her recent discoveries, but her energy levels seemed to be increasing, not decreasing. I mentioned this to her, and she said that she had noticed that as well. "I think I was down before because I thought it was a me problem, but I'm fired up because it's not a me problem, it's a Bob problem." After the requisite fit of laughter that followed every time she said, "Bob problem," she told me that she knew that she would never advance with Bob as her supervisor. She had thought about her options, and she had decided that she was not going to quit; she was going to file an official complaint against Bob, and if the company didn't address it, she would file a gender discrimination suit against Bob and the company.

Louise's decision to take charge of her circumstances created more stress in her life, but the decision was her choice, and the stress that accompanied that decision was her choice as well. After making the decision to file a complaint against Bob, Louise consistently started logging peace levels above six, even though she was dealing with more stress in some ways. And, as her peace increased, she was enjoying the things she could not enjoy before. She told Bob that her school schedule was nonnegotiable and she would not be available at all when time was blocked on her calendar for school. She pushed back against unrealistic deadlines and refused to finish work that he was not completing. Now that she had realized that she had nothing to lose by telling him no, she was quite enthusiastically telling him no on a regular basis.

She also stopped talking to him about her promotion and worked with her HR representative to pull the materials together to lodge her complaint against him. She also contacted a lawyer in case she needed to file a lawsuit. She started having days where she was logging eights and even nines in her peace journal.

This was not the first time that I had seen a woman's peace level increase even as she made decisions that increased her stress. Taking care of ourselves, being in charge of our own lives, is not always about decreasing stress; it's about decreasing the stress we didn't choose.

And…it is also about learning that just as each of us needs to figure out how to create peace and joy for ourselves, we cannot push our definitions of peace and joy on others…no matter how much we believe that the push is rooted in love.

Esme and Her "Louise Problem"

Louise felt so empowered and energized after our work together that she asked me to work with her younger sister, Esme. "I want to pay for Esme to think through her career and life with you. She is so smart and creative, but she is stuck in this dead-end job as an admin at a small company. I've tried to talk to her and push her, but I think it would help her to talk to you." I agreed to talk to Esme and work with her if she wanted to work with me.

Esme reached out and scheduled a call with me the same day that Louise asked me to speak with her. Given her rapid response, I was a little surprised at how quiet and almost detached she seemed when we spoke. She told me about her job as an administrative assistant for the two founders of a small clothing design firm. She told me she enjoyed her job and had become good friends with the founders. I asked her if she would be interested in doing a log for a week to see there were any insights that would be useful for her.

She agreed to do the log, but I was definitely starting to get the feeling that she was doing this for Louise, not for herself. I told her that she didn't need to do the log if she didn't want to, and she just shrugged and said, "No harm in doing it, right? Maybe I will learn a little about myself." Since there was not anything specific she wanted to work on, I asked her to log her peace, joy, acknowledgment, and community levels twice a day in whatever place and format she felt most comfortable.

When we met a couple of weeks later to go over her logs, she told me that she really enjoyed the activity. I smiled when I saw her logs. Her peace, joy, acknowledgment, and community levels were all consistently sevens, eights, and nines. She even had a couple of tens in there. I asked her what, if anything, she had learned about herself. She said she had realized that her community levels were the ones that were most volatile. "I have a few people in my life that don't really get me and I feel like I have to keep standing up for myself and my choices. I noticed that my community score went down when I spent time with these people. Otherwise, my life looks pretty good."

She was quiet for a moment and then softly confided that her sister, Louise, was one of those people. "Louise thinks I should be doing something different in my life. It feels like she is embarrassed about my job. She cuts me off when I tell her that I am really happy, and I make a good living, and I'm financially okay. I like the people at my company. Louise and I are different, and I don't think she'll be happy for me until I'm more like her." I asked her if she had ever shared these thoughts with Louise. She smiled. "Of course, I've talked to her. But Louise is convinced that I need something else. Like I am choosing things because I'm not ambitious or confident enough. She doesn't hear that I'm choosing them because they're what I want."

Esme's logs—the levels and the notes—were thoughtful, self-aware, and self-confident. They showed a lived daily reality that most women were striving for, a reality that Louise was striving for. But, in our world of more achievement, more money, more something, more anything, Esme's choices were not given the weight of true choices. I asked her if she would feel comfortable sharing her logs with her sister. She was not sure if it would make a difference with Louise but agreed to share her logs with her.

I asked Louise if she would feel comfortable sharing her logs with Esme. She said that she was not sure if Esme could really understand the type of stresses she faced, but she also agreed to share her logs.

After several individual communications with Louise and Esme, they agreed to do a joint call with me after reading each other's logs. I told them I had no experience doing a joint call like this, but I was willing to facilitate a dialogue between them focusing on their logs and their next steps.

There were lots of tears on that call (mine included), and we talked about how hard it is for women to create their personal definitions of peace and joy and how much we can ease that difficulty for each other if we push ourselves and each other in the directions we actually want to travel.

Peace is joy at rest.
Joy is peace on its feet.
—Anne Lamott

You, Joyful

Inhale deeply through your nose. Exhale forcefully through your mouth. Repeat a couple of times to center yourself.

Take a piece of paper and write your full name in big block letters. Write your first, middle, and last names. Write any nicknames you go by as well. Use big block letters. Take up as much of the page as possible. Then, sign your name at the very bottom of the page.

Take a deep breath and just look at your name in front of you. Reflect on who this person is. Think of who she was as a little girl. How did she used to write her name then? How did the teenage you sign her name? How has your signature changed over the years?

(The next part is both silly and intensely emotional. It is okay to giggle, cry, roll your eyes, or anything else you feel like doing. Do what you need to fully experience the moment.)

Think of your senior year in high school self. Imagine her in front of you right now. Ask her to tell you what she thinks about your life today. Ask her what she would do differently if she had the resources you have today. Ask her what she thinks about your home, your work, your friends, your wardrobe.

Do not censor what comes up. Listen to what she has to say. Take as long as you need. Thank her for taking the time to have the conversation with you. Let her know that you are about to write her a letter that she will be able to read when she graduates from high school.

Now, turn the paper over and write a letter to the young woman you just connected with. What do you want her to know as she sets off on her various journeys? What do you want her to always remember and prioritize? What do you want her to stay away from? What is she worried about that she needs to let go of because it is never going to matter? What is something she really wants to do that she should go ahead and do, no matter how many people tell her she should not? What is she afraid of that she should not waste any more time fearing? What is one adventure she should definitely take the time to have? Who are some people she should not bother staying in touch with after high school? Who are some people she should make time to stay in touch with?

Add anything else you want to tell this young woman.

Take a few deep breaths when you are done. Read the letter aloud to yourself.

Is there anything that you told your younger self that is actually good advice for you today? Are there things you told her to do that are not too late for you to do...no matter how silly?

We already know what brings us joy. We have just forgotten or hidden those things and activities as we've taken on the responsibilities of adulthood. Reconnecting with our younger selves (for better or for worse) helps us remember what we have forgotten. Peace and joy are within us. They are wholly in our control to create and maintain. The transition from joy to acknowledgment is the journey from being in charge of our inner world to taking charge of our outer world.

Defining Acknowledgment... For You Today

Acknowledgment Defined
Acceptance of the truth or existence of something.
Recognition of the importance or quality of something.
Expression of gratitude or appreciation for something.
Action of showing that one has noticed someone or something.
—Oxford Dictionary

Acknowledgment is half of correction.
—Russian proverb

After peace is present, when the stress we did not choose is blissfully absent, there is room for joy. When joy—the enthusiasm with which we experience the minutia of our days—flows naturally, we begin to experience the itchy need for acknowledgment. We do not always consciously focus on acknowledgment as a want, but the lack of acknowledgment is often felt as an amorphous obstacle to peace and joy or as a biting frustration that keeps us on edge no matter how much we experience peace and joy.

Acknowledgment is one of those "you know it when you feel it" kinds of words that is universally experienced as a deep human need but uniquely understood and defined by each of us in the context of our individual lives. It is a word that kept showing up in my conversations with women about what was missing in their lives. When I started researching acknowledgment several years ago, I noticed that it was often used interchangeably in research with its linguistic relatives—recognition, appreciation, admission, acceptance, and awareness. But women were not using these other words in expressing their wants. *Appreciation* came up a few times, but the others rarely made an appearance.

What I slowly but surely began to understand is that women were not using *acknowledgment* as a synonym or alternative for recognition or appreciation in a focused way. Women were using acknowledgment to mean all the above — recognition, appreciation, admission, acceptance, awareness, and all the stuff in between that makes someone feel like they are seen and heard and valued for all of who they truly are. Wanting to be acknowledged was about women wanting to be seen as human beings who are infinitely bigger than the sums of their parts, worth unimaginably more than the value that is ascribed to them, strong in ways that the world does not yet fully recognize, and nothing short of magical in the ways that they embody the dualities of being inexhaustible and exhausted simultaneously.

Where peace and joy are internal journeys of who we really are, acknowledgment is the first foray into the external world of how we are perceived, regardless of who we really are. The need to be acknowledged is the need for convergence between who we really are and how we are perceived. The greater the gap between the two, the greater the itch for acknowledgment. While this itch of acknowledgment is often rooted in our own individual and personal experiences, there is an undercurrent of pissedoffness that many women feel about the lack of acknowledgment for all women everywhere.

This undercurrent shows up in how deeply we sometimes feel another woman's pain, and also how much joy we experience when we see women take charge of how the world sees them. We do not always perceive this undercurrent consciously, but when it shows up in our lives through experiences or art or music or stories, we viscerally get what that acknowledgment feels like. It is as if the world we live in is paused for a second, and we experience a concentrated dose of what it feels like live in charge.

This undercurrent is what makes certain moments in films about women transcend time and context and become powerful symbols of snatching the acknowledgment that is due yet denied.

Thelma & Louise

The look in Thelma and Louise's eyes at the end of the movie as they decide to "keep on going," grasp each other's hand, and drive the blue 1966 Thunderbird off the cliff into the Grand Canyon. The movie ends with the car in the air, and our experience of reality in that moment is challenged. We know that death is the most probable outcome of their action, but we emotionally react to their decision to be free on their terms.

Waiting to Exhale

Bernadine's fierce expression in *Waiting to Exhale* as she stands beside her cheating husband's BMW, which she has just stuffed with his expensive clothes and shoes, douses the car with lighter fluid, calmly lights a cigarette, takes a long drag, and then flicks the match into the car to set the whole damn thing ablaze. She then takes another drag of her cigarette, pivots elegantly and flicks the cigarette back into the car while she strides away.

Dolores Claiborne

The perfectly coiffed and proper Vera who turns to Dolores in Dolores Claiborne and says with aristocratic diction, *"Sometimes, Dolores, sometimes you have to be a high-riding bitch to survive. Sometimes, being a bitch is all a woman has to hang on to."*

Set It Off

The whole damn movie is that moment.

The Oxford Dictionary uses four primary definitions of acknowledgment:

1. Acceptance of the truth or existence of something.

2. Recognition of the importance or quality of something.

3. The expression of gratitude or appreciation for something.

4. The action of showing that one has noticed someone or something.

Each of the definitions can spark an entirely different path of inquiry and reflection in our journeys to take charge of our lives. While acknowledgment is felt and experienced as one want, it is helpful to ask yourself which definition describes what you want so that you can take the actions that will satisfy these wants.

Reflect on the four definitions above and take a few minutes to write down your responses to the prompts below.

1. Acceptance of the truth or existence of something.
   - *What is one thing you need to accept about yourself today?*
   - *What is one thing you want someone in your life to accept about you today?*

2. Recognition of the importance or quality of something.
   - *What is one thing you need to recognize as important to you today?*

- ► *What is one thing you want someone in your life to recognize as important to you today?*

3. Expression of gratitude or appreciation for something.
   - ► *What is one thing you need to express appreciation for in your life today?*
   - ► *What is one thing you want someone in your life to express appreciation for today?*

4. The action of showing that one has noticed someone or something.
   - ► *What is one action you need to take to notice something important about yourself today?*
   - ► *What is one action you want someone in your life to take to notice something important about you today?*

Shay

I first met Shay when she was a brilliant and charismatic second-year law student. I mentored her throughout law school and the early years of her legal practice at a prestigious large law firm. Shay reached out to me the year before she was to be considered for partnership to brainstorm and strategize what she needed to do to be successfully elected to the firm's partnership.

When I asked her what she perceived as her greatest challenge to being seen as a strong candidate for partnership, she told me that everyone at the firm loved her, but she did not think that they really understood the value that she added to every project. I asked her to reflect on the different definitions of acknowledgment and consider whether she wanted to be recognized for the value she added or if she wanted to be appreciated for the value she added. Did she want someone to express something to her or did she want someone to express something to the partners in the firm? Did it feel like she was not being seen and heard or did it feel like she was being seen and heard but not valued?

As we talked through the various facets of acknowledgment, Shay had a burst of clarity. "I feel seen and heard. I feel valued. They have recognized what I add in my bonuses. But I do not feel like they see my potential beyond what I can do today as an associate. I don't feel like they acknowledge that I have the potential to be a partner." I asked her what this specific acknowledgment would look like and how she knew what it was supposed to look like. Here are the questions I asked her to reflect on and answer:

▷ How will I know if people in my firm are acknowledging that I have the potential to be a partner?

  ► *Who are these people? (Try and name five people.)*

  ► *How will I know that these people specifically are acknowledging my potential to be a partner? What do they need to specifically say, do, or signal for me to know that they are acknowledging my potential to be a partner?*

  ► *When and how did I learn that these are the specific things that people should be saying/doing/signaling to acknowledge my potential to be a partner?*

▷ Could there be other ways for them to acknowledge what I want them to acknowledge that I am not familiar with?

  ► *How could I learn about these additional ways? Who can I talk to?*

  ► *Can I create additional ways? Is that even a thing? How will I know if it's a thing and what can I do if it is a thing? How do I communicate this?*

▷ How does this acknowledgment change or not change what I do today? Tomorrow? Next week? Next month? Next year? Two years from now?

▷ Given my answers to the above, what is the next thing I want to do to ease the tension around not having this acknowledgment?

When we don't feel acknowledged in any area of our lives, the lack of acknowledgment feels very real, but the details of that acknowledgment get blurred into an ominous and amorphous gray cloud that feels all the more intense because of its lack of definition. The less defined something is, the more powerless we feel in trying to negotiate or neutralize it. The questions that Shay worked on answering did not necessarily have clear answers, but they started breaking apart the amorphousness of that cloud so that she could better understand what it was that she really wanted and how she could go about getting it.

Shay took a couple of weeks to brainstorm answers to the questions and realized that she couldn't answer most of the questions on her own. She identified a couple of partners that she trusted in her firm and worked with them to finesse the questions as well as find and create the answers she needed.

Shay's journey was not about getting the acknowledgment she wanted. It was about empowering herself to identify the details of that acknowledgment and why she felt she needed it to feel okay or move forward.

Being in charge in our lives is not about finding easy answers to our problems. It's about empowering ourselves to break down our problems, understanding their significance (or lack thereof) in our lives, and realizing that we can follow the rules, break the rules, or make new rules to solve the problems. Or better yet, realize this "problem" falls in the universe of "not my problem" and walk away feeling lighter.

Shay did not make partner the first year that she was eligible for partnership, but she had built enough relationships and channels of information to know and trust that the decision was a fair one. She worked on the things she needed to, and she made partner the very next year. This part of Shay's story had a happy ending; however, this type of acknowledgment is easier to break down and negotiate than the type of acknowledgment we want when we are hurt because of bullshit we are supposed to put up with simply because we are women. The former is a journey of seeking satisfaction, of feeling recognized and appreciated for your efforts. The latter is a journey of justice, of feeling avenged for harms suffered.

Women have discovered that they cannot rely on men's chivalry to give them justice.
—Helen Keller

Women and girls have always faced hurdles. But that's never stopped us. We've sacrificed, fought, campaigned, succeeded, been knocked back, and succeeded again. In a race for justice, we've leapt over countless obstacles to win our rights.
—Emma Watson

Diana Relearning

As Diana started adjusting to life after being separated from her husband, she noted how difficult it was to wrap her mind around the sense of peace she could now access. "I would sit there lost sometimes because I didn't have to worry about someone saying or doing something hurtful to me. The first time I realized it was peace was when my daughter walked past me as I drank tea on the living room floor and told me that I looked peaceful." The separation was tough. Being a single mother was tougher. Preparing for divorce was something that she couldn't even contemplate in that moment, but the peace created space for her to remember the things that used to bring her joy.

She reconnected with work and remembered how much she enjoyed it. She slowly started reconnecting with friends she had distanced herself from as so many women in abusive relationships do to keep their abusers happy. She reconnected with personal interests and found new interests that sparked her curiosity and wonder.

As the divorce got underway, she became infuriated when she would hear her husband lie about everything he had done to her. She wanted him to acknowledge that he had lied and cheated; she wanted him to acknowledge she had not deserved the way he had treated her. The peace she found early in the separation was suddenly inaccessible to her because she now wanted acknowledgment. She started losing interest in her activities again. She felt discombobulated and stressed all the time…again.

I asked her to write down all the things she wanted to hear him say. Next to each statement she wanted to hear from him, I asked her to estimate the probability of him actually saying that to her. As she was doing the exercise, she rolled her eyes and said, "He is a liar. Even if he says the things I want him to say, I would never believe him because he is a liar."

Although Diana had done the work to create the peace she needed, the need for acknowledgment from him that he had wronged her kept pulling her back into the same deadly cycle she had worked so hard to escape.

Her search for acknowledgment would deny her peace and her quest for peace would not give her the acknowledgment she wanted from this one particular person who had hurt her. She had to pick which she wanted more, peace or acknowledgment, because she couldn't have both, at least not in the way she had defined acknowledgment.

The acknowledgment we want when we want unfairness or even abuse to be recognized, admitted, corrected, or otherwise accounted for is not easy to get, and the search for that acknowledgment comes at a price that may be too high to pay.

Therein lies the irony in wanting acknowledgment from someone who wronged you—the very thing that led them to wrong you will keep them from acknowledging the wrong you suffered. The author Jyoti Patel writes "Always choose silence with liars, cheaters, cowards or spineless people. Don't ask them any kind of questions. You don't have to give them any kind of answers or explanations. Ignore, avoid, stay away."

The want for this type of acknowledgment is not a bad thing, but we need to be strategic about who we want that acknowledgment from and the energy we are willing to spend to chase it. While acknowledgment for recognition and appreciation can come from people who are benefiting from or evaluating your efforts, acknowledgment for injustice cannot come (except in some rare circumstances) from the people who committed the injustice. This type of acknowledgment most likely will come from your community of sisters or from yourself, not from the harm doer. The acknowledgment from your community or yourself will not feel like justice, but it is acknowledgment, and it will help you heal. And when you heal, you take charge of your life again. And when you take charge of your life again, you experience the world differently.

None of the powerful scenes from *Thelma & Louise*, *Waiting to Exhale*, *Dolores Claiborne*, and *Set It Off* show justice being served. *We are not inspired by these moments because the wrongdoers acknowledged how fucked-up they were; we are inspired because the women redefined acknowledgment to be something they could give themselves.*

I asked Diana to watch *Dolores Claiborne*. After she watched it, she sent me an email that said, *"He used to call me a bitch. He still does. I've been wanting him to tell me that he shouldn't have called me a bitch, that I'm not a bitch. If Vera is right and that sometimes being a bitch is all a woman has to hang onto, I will be the best damn bitch he has ever encountered. I need to figure what the hell a high-riding bitch is, though. That does sound fun."*

"Every day I realize more and more that if the world is going to change at all, it is going to change through the healing of the victims. Abusers run the show, they insist on and instigate cover-ups, they misuse their power, teach things falsely out of the desire to control but as the victims heal and get stronger, the abusers will not be able to hide behind the fog that they create."
—*Darlene Ouimet*

Defining Community...For You Today

Here's to strong women.
May we know them.
May we be them.
May we raise them.
—*Anonymous*

Women's friendships are like a renewable source of power.
—*Jane Fonda*

We have all heard of our brain's "fight or flight" response when we are in danger. But most of us have not heard about our brain's "tend and befriend" response. While men and women both experience "fight or flight," "tend and befriend" occurs primarily just in women. When the threat/stress system is activated in our bodies, men and women produce adrenaline and cortisol—this is what gives our bodies the oomph we need to flee fast or fight hard. When we experience chronic stress, an extra push of cortisol and adrenaline overwhelms our response systems, and we can have a third response—freeze. Every time we experience stress, our minds and bodies work together to figure out whether we should fight, flee, or freeze.

But something interesting happens in women soon after this infusion of cortisol and adrenaline. We produce oxytocin, and oxytocin immediately reduces the amount of cortisol and adrenaline in our bodies. Oxytocin, sometimes non-ironically referred to as the cuddle hormone, neutralizes our fight, flee, or freeze response and activates our tend and befriend response, an instinct that causes us to tend to what matters to us (usually our children and homes) and reach out to—befriend—women who will support us as we deal with the stress. When women are stressed, we may sometimes fight, flee, or freeze, but more often than not, we get our shit organized and rally our sisters. Community is our response to threat and stress.

People much more knowledgeable than me in the sciences of anthropology, neurological evolution, and hormonal impact on behavior have written about why women evolved from the fight or flee response to the tend and befriend response. My explanation of this evolution is a gross simplification of the science, so please take it with a grain of salt.

Women's threat response transitioned from fight or flight to tend and befriend because we didn't really have a choice. Evolutionarily speaking, most of us are descendants from hunter-gatherer peoples among whom men were usually the hunters and women were the gatherers. Men went off to hunt for food and protect against predators (of the animal and human varieties), and women took care of the children, the living spaces, and transformed the fruits of the hunting and gathering into food, clothing, and other usable resources for everyone.

In this evolutionary flashback, the fight or flight response made sense for the men: It activated their abilities to fight back or outrun threats to their safety coming from animals or male hunters from neighboring villages. Men were equipped and trained to fight or flee these attacks. The primary threats to women, unfortunately, were the men—in their own homes and villages as well as men from other villages who raped and pillaged as part of their hunting and protecting activities.

When women were threatened by men—in historic and contemporary times—the fight or flight response wasn't very effective, because we usually cannot outfight or outrun the threats. I imagine that it didn't take too many generations before women's brains evolved to the more effective response of organizing and fighting back collectively. If a village was attacked—regardless of whether the men of that village were there to fight back or not—the women needed to move quickly to corral and protect the children, themselves, and resources such as livestock and food. They wouldn't be strong enough to fight back, and they wouldn't be fast or nimble enough to flee with the children in tow.

Women could protect themselves if they had their shit together and if they fought back collectively. We don't have to deal with protecting ourselves from marauders in the same way anymore, but the greatest threat to women—physically and emotionally—continues to be men. As Dr. Kirtly Parker Jones at the University of Utah summed up in 2014, "What's the biggest health threat to women? It's intimate partner violence. One in three women on the planet will be raped or beaten in her lifetime... Of all the women murdered in the U.S., about one-third were killed by a domestic partner, and the rate of non-lethal abuse is much higher than that."[10] As the Australian news put it in 2019, "If you're a young woman, the biggest risk to your well-being is not cancer or an automobile accident. That risk is right in front of you—in the form of your bloke."[11] The World Health Organization continues to sound the alarm on violence against women by stating in March 2019, "Violence against women remains devastatingly pervasive and starts alarmingly young...one in three women, around 736 million, are subjected to physical or sexual violence by an intimate partner or sexual violence from a non-partner—a number that has remained largely unchanged over the past decade."[12]

When it comes to women's responses to the actual threats we face, fighting back or fleeing never did protect or save us. So, we evolved, creating our superpower of community. Community is our defense mechanism against threats, and it's our renewable energy source for the power to forge ahead.

Any time women come together with a collective intention, it's a powerful thing. Whether it's sitting down making a quilt, in a kitchen preparing a meal, in a club reading the same book, or around the table playing cards, or planning a birthday party, when women come together with a collective intention, magic happens.
—*Phylicia Rashad*

There is a special place in hell for women who don't help other women.
—*Madeleine K. Albright*

Given that community is our superpower, it's not surprising that it is an important need in our lives and it is painful when that need is not met. After peace, joy, and acknowledgment wants are satisfied to reasonable levels, a strong community of women rounds out the foundation of what it takes to be in charge of our lives. It is important to note that when women said they wanted a community of women, they didn't see this community as a replacement for strong relationships with men. Women described this community of women as an extension of themselves, like a stand of aspen trees growing above ground as individuals but deeply interconnected below ground by an extensive root system that nourishes and strengthens the collective.

Anna

Anna, a junior engineer at a power company, had been with the company for about eight months and was thriving at work. She loved her team and the team leader. Although she was the only woman on the team, she didn't feel excluded or unappreciated. The team was close, and they often socialized after work and on the weekends at each other's homes and with each other's families. Anna came from a large family, and she didn't get home often, so she loved the connection to her team's families. Anna and the other junior engineer on the team were the only ones who were single and without kids, and they were relentlessly hounded by the rest of the team members and their families to "find someone, settle down, and start a family." "You are not getting any younger!" was a phrase she had heard at least a couple of times every week when she first started.

After a week of multiple late nights due to a particularly volatile project, the team went out to a local bar for drinks on Friday. Anna had a couple of drinks with the guys but begged off when they ordered a third round. She was tired, and she wanted to get home and go to sleep. The other junior engineer said that he was tired as well and offered to share a taxi with Anna because they lived just a couple of blocks from each other.

Anna nodded off when she got in the taxi, and she suddenly awoke, feeling her coworker's hands on her body and his lips on her lips. She tried to push him off, but he was stronger than her, and she couldn't scream because his mouth was on hers. When he started to unbutton her shirt and push up her skirt, she panicked and started kicking the taxi driver's seat to get his attention. The taxi driver ignored her kicks for a couple of minutes, but when she continued to kick at a frenetic pace, he finally pulled over. Leveraging her coworker's momentary surprise, she opened the taxi door and stumbled onto the sidewalk. He got out and came toward her.

Anna's brain couldn't process what was happening, and she stood on the sidewalk, trying to button up her shirt and straighten her skirt. As he came toward Anna, two women stepped in front of her. "I work with her," he told them. "She had a lot to drink. I'm checking to make sure she's okay." One of the women looked back at Anna struggling with her clothes and shook her head in disbelief. She addressed him directly. "Unless she says otherwise, you are going to leave her alone, and we will make sure she's okay." The woman turned to Anna and asked if she wanted him to stay. Anna shook her head vehemently. He protested a little, but he left when he saw that the women were not going to let him anywhere near Anna.

After he left, one of the women led Anna to a nearby bench and waited with her while the other went to the coffee shop across the street to get her a cup of hot chocolate. Anna was shivering violently, and she couldn't stomach the thought of drinking anything. The woman gently told her that she was in shock and to sip the hot chocolate slowly to warm up or at least just hold the cup to warm her hands. They asked Anna if she wanted to call anyone or call the police, and Anna shook her head. Then, they sat down next to her on the sidewalk and waited with her.

An hour or so passed. Anna slowly started registering where she was and the women who were waiting silently with her on the bench. She was still shivering, but she felt like she could get up and walk the few blocks to her apartment. The women suggested that they walk with her just in case she wasn't okay. Anna insisted that she was fine, and they insisted that they would walk with her. Anna was grateful for the support, and she thanked them for everything they had done.

When they reached her apartment building, Anna felt a lot calmer and stronger, and she told them she would be fine. One of the women quietly said, "He said you worked together. Is that true?" Anna nodded, and the woman said, "This isn't over yet if you have to see him on Monday. Don't try and tough it out and do it on your own. You are going to need support to get through this." Anna nodded and the women left.

When Anna walked into her apartment, she fell to the floor and started crying. She called her sister, who lived across the state line from where Anna lived, and told her what happened as she sobbed. Her sister stayed on the phone until Anna's sobs had subsided a little and told her that she was going to get in her car and drive to her, and she wanted Anna to stay on the phone with her for the three to four hours that the drive would take.

Anna's sister is a good friend of mine, and I had met Anna before, but I didn't know her well. Anna's sister knew that I had done sexual assault victim advocacy work for years and convinced Anna to talk to me. They called me together, and Anna told me what happened. I talked to Anna for a long time that night, and I gave her some resources to help her navigate the situation however she wanted to. I then asked her if we could touch base daily, even if for just a few minutes, so that I could support her choices and experiences at work.

Anna initially said that she would be fine with work. She said that she would take the weekend to pull herself together and she would be professional at the office. She knew she wouldn't be socializing with her team the way she used to, but she really felt that she could be professional...until she received a text from her team leader on Sunday afternoon. "Heard taxi share didn't go so well. He said he was an ass. Shake it off. Both of you had been drinking."

Anna forwarded the text to me and her sister as soon as she received it. The three of us got on a call, and Anna just cried for a few minutes. Then, she said, "I really thought we were like a family. He didn't even call me to hear what I had to say before he sent that text." Her sister and I didn't say anything. We didn't need to.

That's the superpower of women's communities. You don't need to explain or justify. You can just ask women to be there so that you know you aren't in it alone.

On Sunday night, Anna decided that she wasn't ready to face anything at work, so she sent her team leader an email to let him know that she wasn't feeling well, and she would be taking a few days off. On Tuesday, she called me and said, "Okay, I'm ready to do something. What do I do?" I told her "First, you get your team together. Then, you play the game you want to play, and you win."

The team was a group of seven women who either Anna or her sister trusted implicitly, and we sat on Anna's living room floor with large goblets of wine, and we planned. It was going to be a multi-pronged approach; the group text that Anna's sister started with all of us was called #TeamAnna.

Anna filed a report with her company's Human Resources on Thursday morning because she wanted a formal complaint on the record even though she didn't think they would do anything. Right after she filed the report, she called her team leader and told him that his text to her on Sunday was not only inappropriate, but it also was not compliant with company policy. She told him exactly what happened and let him know that she would not work on the same team as the guy that assaulted her, so either she or her assailant would have to be transferred to a different team. Her team leader asked her if she wanted to come in and talk to him in person, and she replied that she would only do that if her assailant had been transferred.

Anna learned from HR that hers wasn't the first complaint filed against this guy; two sexual misconduct complaints had been filed against him before Anna's, and he had been with the company less than a year. Anna knew that her team leader would have been apprised of the complaints, and she realized that, knowing what he knew, he had still let Anna get into a cab with this guy and sent her a "Both of you had been drinking" text.

Anna transferred from that team to a team with more women, and she ended up leaving the company within a year of her assault. Her assailant still works at the company. She and I stay in touch, and she has told me several times that she would never have had the strength and courage to deal with it the way she had if she hadn't had #TeamAnna.

Without community, it is very difficult for women to maintain the peace, joy, and acknowledgment they work so hard to secure. I have often quoted Madeleine Albright's quip "There is a special place in hell for women who don't help other women," because women helping women is a lifeline to each woman, a source of collective power that overrides the systems that don't work in her favor. Whenever the power to control their lives has been taken or kept from women, one of the tactics used to keep women from fighting back is to shame, scare, or bully us into isolation. I'm not suggesting that every woman in your life is a part of your community, but your community is bigger than you realize.

You & Your Community

Inhale deeply through your nose. Exhale forcefully through your mouth. Repeat a couple of times to center yourself.

Take a piece of unlined paper and draw one big circle in the middle. Then draw five to seven random circles of different sizes inside the big circle. Don't worry about what it's supposed to look like or if you are doing it right. Just make one big circle with five to seven smaller circles inside.

Look at the smaller circles and imagine that each of those circles is a problem you are dealing with or trying to solve in your life. You can pick the ones that are toughest for you, or just any five problems. Add more circles if you need to write down more problems. Just make sure they are all inside the big circle. A circle cannot contain just a person's name...add whatever it is that makes dealing with this person a problem.

Take a look at your handiwork. Do you need to add another circle or two within the larger circle? Do you need to reframe or reword any of the problems?

Once you are done with the problems, take a deep breath in and blow it out purposefully. Take out a new piece of paper for this part of the journey. Now, start thinking of all the women in your life who make your life more peaceful, more joyful, more of all the good things. From bloggers that inspire you to your besties to the barista who makes your cup of coffee so perfectly every morning, to your sisters to your colleagues at work and on and on, don't stop until you come up with at least thirty names. Yep, thirty. That's a lot of names, and you will most likely get frustrated, but you cannot go on to the next part until you come up with thirty names.

Sometimes when I do this exercise, I get to thirty very quickly, and other times, my list is filled with people like Beyoncé and Pink, because my life was better in that moment after listening to "Survivor" and "So What." Don't judge yourself. Just get to thirty names.

Now for the fun part. Take out the paper with the problems on it. Now, you are going to carefully and in your best handwriting write the names of the thirty women you listed in the larger circle between the circles with the problems in them. If you think of more people as you are writing, please add them!

Once you are done, take a deep breath in, exhale, and look at your masterpiece. That larger circle is your community. Now, ask yourself if those problems floating in that sea of powerful, strong, amazing women have any chance of surviving.

You are not facing any of those problems by yourself. You have a community. Even if you think you don't, you do. There is at least one woman in your life who either has your back or will have your back if you ask.

Those problems are stressful and painful and frustrating, and they are no match for you and your community.

I cannot imagine where I would be today without my sisters, my community of strong, passionate, loyal, badass women. They have held me up when I wasn't strong enough to stand on my own, and they have kicked my butt into motion when I got stuck. In 1697, the poet William Congreve coined the phrase that has colloquially become "hell hath no fury like a woman scorned." What William really did not understand about women is that the woman scorned is not the one that people should be scared of—instead, the truer observation is that *hell hath no fury like a sister of a woman scorned.* While the woman scorned is crying, her sister is plotting.

∗Anna∗

An Epilogue

#TeamAnna had Anna's back as she transitioned from victim to survivor. She never had to wonder if she was in it by herself, and even in those moments she had to face alone, she knew that someone on #TeamAnna was waiting by the phone if she wanted to talk or vent or cry.

What Anna did not know is that while she was meeting with Human Resources, filing a complaint, and meeting with a lawyer, her sister and I "ran into" the guy that assaulted her, and we had a quick conversation with him to let him know that while Anna was upset and scared right now, #TeamAnna was pissed off to the max and ready—itching—for a fight. When he opened his mouth to talk, Anna's sister shook her head as she shushed him. "It's in your best interest if I never hear your voice or see your face again."

He opened his mouth to speak again. She shushed him again and said, "I really want to hurt you. I won't because it won't help Anna right now. But I really want to hurt you. I've made a long list of all the ways I can fuck up your life for the rest of your life. So, you are going to never speak to me or Anna or anyone else connected to Anna again. Nod if you understand me."

He nodded and rushed out of the coffee shop where we had "run into" him.

Fight or flight has nothing on tend and befriend.

Community is our superpower.

I would be remiss if I didn't address that nagging thought that many of you may have had as you read the previous section. *Not all women are nice to women. At times, it's women who are the worst to other women. Women knock down other women because of insecurities. So on and so forth.*

I do not deny any of that. Some of the worst moments of my life have been inflicted on me by other women, but even in those women-caused painful moments, it was my community of sisters that got me through those times. Women are not universally kind to other women, but those unkind, non-communal women are nowhere near the majority. They may be louder at times than the rest of us, but they don't represent the majority of women any more than the asshole that assaulted Anna represents all men.

Men don't have the monopoly on being assholes, and women don't have the monopoly on being kind. That said, the reality for most women is that we have to navigate a world where the rules weren't made by us, for us, or in our best interests. That navigation is most likely to be successful for women if it's a collective effort.

(RE)CONNECTING THE DOTS

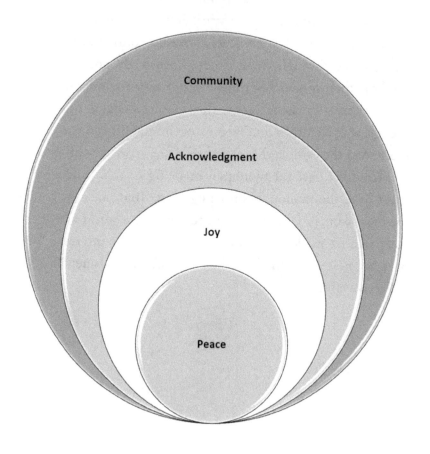

Peace. Joy. Acknowledgment. Community. These were the common threads of wants woven through all the different women's stories. The specifics of how those wants were expressed changed from woman to woman, but the core wants were surprisingly consistent. One woman yearned for a promotion at work because she wanted acknowledgment, and another yearned for a promotion so that she could enjoy the day-to-day of her work more. One woman's vacation goal was a trip to Mexico for peace and quiet on a beach, and another woman's vacation goal was to enjoy running a marathon in a new country. What we want is similar across our differences, but how we get what we want is different for each of us.

Self-concordant goals help us identify our unique paths to peace, joy, acknowledgment, and community. Reflect on these questions as we transition from "what we want" to "how we make that happen." Remember to answer the questions according to what feels most right for the real you today.

▷ What is one activity that consistently brings you peace?

▷ What is one activity that consistently brings you joy?

▷ What is one activity in which you feel recognized and appreciated?

▷ What is one way in which you connect with your community regularly?

Before you go any further in this book, go do one of those activities right now. Yes, right now!

ACTIONS
TO GET IN CHARGE

STOP & SUBTRACT

If you want to fly,
you got to give up the shit that weighs you down.
—Toni Morrison, Song of Solomon

Learn how to exhale, the inhale will take care of itself.
—Carla Melucci Ardito

The first step in taking charge of our lives and ensuring that our goals are self-concordant and are pathways to peace, joy, acknowledgment, and community is to stop...to subtract...to exhale.

Did you know that most problems we have with breathing—asthma, COPD, bronchitis, etc.—deal with our inability to exhale? When we say we are short of breath or having trouble breathing, more often than not, we are having problems exhaling, not inhaling. Obstructive lung disease, the umbrella disease for asthma, COPD, bronchitis, etc., happens when we inhale, process the oxygen, create carbon dioxide as a by-product of our oxygen processing, and then can't constrict our lungs enough to exhale, to get rid of the carbon dioxide so that we can inhale and take in more oxygen.

Our bodies, minds, and hearts intuitively know how to take things in, but finding peace, joy, acknowledgment, and community require our exhaling skillsets to be as strong as our inhaling tendencies. It's easier to take in than to let go, to hoard than to release, to say *yes* than to say *no*; however, if we take in and hoard and say *yes* without letting go and releasing and saying *no*, we will get sick. We will get overwhelmed, burned out, stressed out, and frustrated on every level.

Being in charge of our lives begins with letting go...exhaling... things that no longer serve us well. Even if everything in our lives is there because we put it there purposefully, we will still get overwhelmed and burned out because we aren't balancing the taking in and putting out.

When I first started researching this concept over ten years ago, I immediately thought of *Waiting to Exhale.* It is human instinct to inhale and to hold our breath, but it seems that we women need to learn (or maybe remember) how to exhale.

An exhalation is an act of letting go, of purging the unnecessary to make room for the necessary. Our calendars, our to-do lists, our bucket of responsibilities at home and at work, and even our closets need to exhale as much as they inhale. One of my friends has a rule for her closet that I use for my closet and my life—one out, one in. Every time she wants to buy something that will go into her closet, she has to take one thing and gift it, donate it, or trash it before she buys the new thing. Ever since I started applying that rule to my closet about two years ago, I have not had to make time to clean out or organize my closet.

One out, one in.

When I saw how well this worked with my closet, I started experimenting with its application in my calendar, in my to-do list, and in my responsibilities at work as well as in other professional and personal areas of my life. It's a profound idea than can help us understand how much of our overwhelm is due to adding things without subtracting anything. I started applying it with clients and quickly realized that there is a common reason that women just keep inhaling, and we don't exhale until life forces us to—we don't want to be seen as quitters.

Helene

Helene was a senior manager in a nonprofit organization that worked on civil rights issues for people who were incarcerated. I had been working with her to create a self-advocacy curriculum for women when she told me that the executive director of the organization had announced his retirement, and the board of directors had asked her if she would be interested in being considered for the position. "If I say I'm interested, I don't think they will do a search. They want me to do this. I just don't know if I can. I don't want to fail. I cannot take on more than what I'm doing now."

We first confronted the fear of failure she had expressed. I asked her to list all the things she felt could lead to failure. She made a list of about ten things, ranging from she wouldn't have enough fundraising time to a lack of time to screen new hires effectively to insufficient time to adequately connect with the board. Almost all of her fears of failure were rooted in not having enough time; she did not lack confidence in her abilities to do the job. I've noticed that people, especially women, fear failure when they think about all the additional things they need to do if they take on more responsibility…but they don't think about what they will release or delegate. Of course, it feels overwhelming if you are thinking about inhaling more and more without exhaling anything.

I asked Helene to create two columns on a page and write "Executive Director" on top of the left column and "Senior Manager" on top of the right column. I asked her to put her name above the "Senior Manager" heading and the current executive director's name over that heading. Her assignment was to list out all the responsibilities and tasks relegated to each role. I asked her to get as detailed as possible.

When we sat down to go over these lists, I asked her to cross out the Executive Director's name and write in her name. Then, I asked her to scratch out her name and write in "new senior manager—need to promote or hire." She looked at the lists, and then it slowly hit her. If she were doing the executive director's job, she would not be doing a lot of what she was currently doing. "I was picturing doing what I'm doing right now and what he's doing right now, wasn't I? I need to hire a me." She thought about it a bit longer and said "Now that I think about it, I'd make a better him than he does. I already do a lot of what should be his job. The person I hire wouldn't be as busy as I am because I would be doing more than he does."

One out, one in. For every responsibility she was taking on, she had to first shed one responsibility. Lists like this can be powerful visual tools that help you see what your fears won't let you—that you aren't going to be doing more. If you do it right, you are just going to be doing different things than you did before. Once Helene neutralized her "I won't have enough time to do it all" fear of failure, her confidence in her abilities and her excitement about new ideas for the organization kicked in.

Never Ever Quit,
but Stop What Isn't Working

When my firm, Nextions, turned 15 years old in 2014, we published a book entitled *15 Lessons in 15 Years*. We brainstormed all that we had learned, and we had no idea then that these lessons would become some of the foundations of our research on individual energy management. We just thought we were channeling our most challenging experiences into pithy lessons learned.

"Never ever quit, but stop doing something if it isn't working," and "Letting go is often harder than hanging on," were two of the first lessons in *15 Lessons in 15 Years*. I had learned these lessons multiple times in my personal and professional lives, and my team and I had learned these lessons repeatedly through various projects that we had undertaken and with several of the clients with whom we had worked, some of whom we had to fire because of their behavior. (You would be shocked at what people feel comfortable saying to women who work in the areas of inclusion, equity, and diversity.)

These two lessons, critical to being in charge of your own energy on your paths to peace, joy, acknowledgment, and community, both stem from pushing back against the rigid social messages that quitting is always bad and letting go is what you do when you cannot hang on any longer. Think of the oft-quoted one-liners such as "Winners never quit, and quitters never win," by Vince Lombardi; or "The struggle is temporary, quitting lasts forever," by Lance Armstrong; or "The difference between winning and losing is most often...not quitting," by Walt Disney; or "When you get to the end of your rope, tie a knot and hang on," by Franklin D. Roosevelt. "Hang in there," "hang on," and "don't give up," are the phrases we reflexively repeat when people tell us they are struggling or suffering. I've had these messages drummed into my brain throughout my life—quitting was what weak people did, but the strong people were the ones who were hanging on.

The problem with truisms like these is that quitting and hanging on are rooted in very specific definitions of success and failure, of winning and losing. A football game, for example, is played for 60 minutes, and there is a clear winner or loser at the end of the game. So, it makes sense for a coach like Vince Lombardi to encourage his players to not quit until the game is over. Similarly, when reflecting on the Tour de France, a daunting bicycle race of 2,000 miles, it would make sense for Lance Armstrong (with all of his performance enhancing challenges) to say the struggle—the muscular exhaustion around mile 1,000—is temporary, but quitting—leaving the race at mile 1,000—lasts forever. If you suffer through the pain of mile 1,000, you will eventually get to the end, mile 2,000.

Yes, it makes absolute sense to tell someone to hang on in the middle of an athletic endeavor, a military battle, a health crisis, or even an academic journey. But it only makes sense because the end—success—is clearly defined: winning the game or battle, getting through an illness, or matriculation from an academic program.

What happens when success isn't clearly defined? Or if you didn't get to play a role in how success was defined? Or if there is actually no definition of success at all? Imagine if someone was running a race in which the finish line had never been determined, and you told them to never quit, to just hang in there. How long do they hang on? When do they get to stop? Do they just have to keep running forever? It sounds silly in this context, but most workplaces ask people to work in ways where no one can tell you where the finish line is, what winning looks like, or what success feels like—yet they tell you to hang on and hang in there every day.

Of course, badass women do not quit! They don't quit when they are working toward goals that they want to achieve. But when they find themselves hustling for something that they never actively consented to achieving, they do let go of stuff that's not working for them. And they know when to hang on and when to let go because they stop to define success for themselves; they set their own finish lines and their own milestones. They stop doing things that no longer serve their needs or feel good, and they only hang on when they determine something is worth hanging on for.

Michaela

Michaela, a Latina executive at a large corporation, is a badass by anyone's measure. She grew up in poverty, put together multiple scholarships to get into and graduate from college (the first person in her family on her mom's and dad's sides), and worked as an analyst at a major consulting firm before going back to school to get her MBA. She worked at another consulting firm for a few years before being hired as a vice president at a Fortune 1000 Company. She had just been promoted to senior vice president when she was referred to me for coaching.

In the first coaching session I had with Michaela, I asked her to tell me something about herself that would give me a real glimpse into who she was. She giggled and told me about the first paycheck she received when she was an analyst. She had opened the envelope, seen the check, and started hyperventilating. "I had never seen that much money in one place that belonged to me. I didn't want to cash the check or deposit it. I just wanted to stare at it. I called my mom and told her that I didn't want to cash this paycheck! My mom told me to call HR and tell them I lost the check. She said they would issue me a new one, and I could keep this one. I did just that." Does she still have that check? "Absolutely, I do. It's in my nightstand drawer. It's a bit beat up and wrinkled, but I still look at it often. It's a symbol of my journey from impossible to possible."

This badass woman, a senior vice president at a Fortune 1000 company, was given the feedback from senior leadership that, to advance at the company, she needed to work on…time management.

Knowing the work I was doing on energy management for women, her HR business partner referred her to me instead of to their usual time management coach.

"I'm terrible at managing my time," Michaela told me when I asked her what she wanted to get out of the coaching sessions. "I'm late a lot, to meetings, with some deadlines, responding to emails, all that stuff. I need to get better at it to get ahead."

Before we figured out how she could manage her time better or if time management were even the problem, we needed to figure out how she actually spent her time. She agreed to keep an hourly journal for five days, Monday through Friday. It would be an informal but detailed accounting of her time from when she woke up to when she went to sleep. She used a time-entry app on her phone for her ease (clients have used everything from good old-fashioned analog pen and paper to apps on their phones to their work calendars). I asked her to put in as much information as possible—who a meeting was with, if it was a phone call, a video call, a live meeting, etc., organic run-ins with people that took more than five minutes, daily commutes, time in an airport, time on a flight, prepping for a meeting, social time, and so on. In addition to a careful accounting of her time, I asked her to rate her energy level at the end of every entry from one to ten, with one being **"NEED A NAP NOW"** and ten being **"FEELING AMAZING."**

It sounds complicated, but it's a "do your best, and let's just see what it tells us" kind of exercise. No, you will not do it perfectly, and yes, whatever you do log is helpful. Michaela's log looked something like this:

MONDAY

- ▷ 8-8:45 scheduled call with John: 3
- ▷ 8:45-9:15 returned Al's call from yesterday: 4

- ▷ Late for my 9, 9:15 to 10, check-in with team on project updates: 5
- ▷ 10 to 10:30, meeting with Steve, didn't have time to prep, winged it, not perfect but okay: 4
- ▷ 10:30-10:45 ran downstairs to Starbucks to get a bagel, long line but food: 6
- ▷ 11:15-1 worked on presentation with Stace, not happy with what Stace has done, lots of excuses: 3
- ▷ Double booked at 1, went to each meeting for 30 minutes: 5
- ▷ 3-4 emergency meeting with vendor: 5
- ▷ 4:30-6:30 leadership team meeting, was late for the meeting because mom called, dad's having a hard time breathing: 3
- ▷ I should go home for a few days but bad timing right now. Maybe this weekend.
- ▷ Canceled drinks with C. Was looking forward to going out with him. But need to make sure that I'm organized for tomorrow: 4
- ▷ Worked out 8-9 and steamed at gym: 7
- ▷ 9-11 Worked on stuff for tomorrow, ate a quick dinner, called mom, had a couple of glasses of wine: 7

TUESDAY

- ▷ 5:15 woke up, don't know when I fell asleep yesterday: 6
- ▷ 6:30 in the office, EA is sick today: 4
- ▷ 7:00 meeting with John, tried to get him to make decisions, he rambled, meeting ran late until 8:30. Was supposed to done at 7:45: 3
- ▷ 8:30-9:30 meeting with team, they had to wait for me because I ran over, K is angry, ugh: 2
- ▷ 10-12 call w/Asian partners, the time was messed up...they aren't happy: 3

- ▷ 12-1 meeting with Diversity team, sponsoring a group, wish I could do more, just don't have time: 5
- ▷ 1-3 lunch and prep for meeting with M: 5
- ▷ 3 called mom, need to go home: 2
- ▷ 46 Steve pissed about submitted estimates, T isn't taking responsibility, I had no control on this: 2
- ▷ 7 home, too tired to work out, ate dinner: 3
- ▷ 8-10:30 worked, head hurting, Advil, bed: 2

You get the picture! I was exhausted after reading about just five days of her life. I had no idea how she lived at this pace every day. The first thing we did was go over how infrequently she reported anything over a five. As we were doing this, she said, "I know! If I could just get better with time management, I would have more eights and nines, right?"

Actually, not right. The more we dug into her schedule, the more obvious it became that she was not in charge of her schedule. Almost 70% of her daily schedule was consistently put on her calendar by someone else. She—and by extension her EA—did not have a screening or organizing mechanism by which commitments showed up on her calendar. The majority of her calls and meetings had no agendas, and there were several meetings to which she was invited simply because people felt better when she was present because she "managed conflict in conversations so well," as one of her colleagues told her. This colleague was also one of the people who told Michaela that she needed to manage her time better if she wanted to advance into senior leadership.

It was impossible for her to better manage how other people were managing her time. So, the first thing we did was screen her calendar for the next week to identify what she needed to remove. Her calendar was inhaling every single day and not given any chance to exhale!

This was difficult for her because she did not want to tell other people that she didn't have time for them. She felt bad about canceling meetings even though she acknowledged she needed the time for other things. It was a rough couple of hours, but we ended up reducing her commitments by about 20%. Sometimes, letting go is harder than hanging on...not because we don't have the strength to hang on, but because we never gave ourselves permission to let go.

Next, we tagged everything on her calendar for the next week that needed an agenda in advance and sent sample scripts to her EA to set/get agendas and have them entered into the calendar so that they were visible for all attendees. (I personally believe that all calls and meetings should have agendas, however informal, because if you don't know where you are going, how will you know if you got there?)

She kept a log for that next week, and she started seeing how having less—but more important—stuff on her calendar (with agendas!) was making her be and feel more productive. Then, we dove into the work of classifying everything in her day as an energy gain or an energy drain. We cannot always get rid of energy drains but if we identify what exactly is draining our energy, we can find ways to neutralize the drain or even turn an energy drain into an energy gain.

Michaela's father was ill, and she was worried about her mother, her father's medical care, and her parents' financial affairs. Her calls to her mom between her work calls and meetings were a source of energy drain in her life because the calls always took longer than she anticipated, and she always hung up feeling worried about her parents and guilt-ridden for not being at home with them. We spent one full session on just this issue. Michaela constantly felt that she wasn't showing her parents how much she loved them and that she wasn't doing all she could for them. We also identified that squeezing in calls to her mother was very stressful because she wasn't focused when she talked to her mom, and it was difficult for her to refocus on work after these conversations.

She decided to create more structure around her conversations with her mother in a way that created more energy for her and her mom. She started by asking her mom what her parents truly needed. Her mother tearfully told her that the ways in which Michaela was able to help financially was allowing both of her parents to focus on her father's health. Michaela and her mom created a plan to videocall every morning and every evening. They also created a family calendar so that all of Michaela's father's appointments were online for Michaela to see. They talked about how Michaela could do one-day trips to see them instead of long weekends. The scheduled video calls made her feel closer to her parents, and she didn't have to do the difficult transitions at work. She also realized that it had never occurred to her to do one-day trips, because she thought her parents would think she was being rude or callous if she did that. But not only were her parents excited about her one-day trips, they were her mom's suggestion!

We also identified some nonnegotiable energy gainers like working out, investing time in her newly blossoming romantic relationship, and connecting regularly with her friends. The changes weren't easy (okay, they were really hard for her at first), but after a few weeks of managing her energy as carefully as she managed her business goals, we started seeing more eights, nines, and even a few tens on her daily logs.

The idea of being in charge hit home for her when her EA told her how much she enjoyed telling Michaela's colleague—the one who asked her to be in meetings so that everyone felt better and then turned around and criticized her for how she managed her time—that while Michaela would be happy to meet with him anytime he wanted, she would be sending someone from her team for meetings where her presence wasn't necessary.

Michaela never needed to learn how to manage her time. She needed to focus on what did not need to take up her time. She needed to learn to be in charge of her time in a way that created peace and joy in her life.

Stop by Default, Start by Choice

A designer knows he has achieved perfection not when there is nothing left to add,
but when there is nothing left to take away.
—Antoine de Saint-Exupéry

Human brains love default settings. Research consistently demonstrates that if you want to change human behavior, you need to make the desired behavior the one that requires less effort than the undesired behavior. The desired behavior should be the default, and the undesired behavior would be the one that people have to go out of their way to choose. For example, when websites ask people to opt in to receive marketing materials, only 29% actively opt in, but when websites ask people to opt out of receiving marketing materials, 51% don't opt out.[13] If you make the *yes* a choice, only 29% will say *yes*, but if you make the *no* a choice, only 49% will say *no*, resulting in a 51% *yes*.

If you are cleaning out your closet, even with the most aggressive of intentions, you will only get rid of about 15 to 20% if you're just looking for what to discard. But if you take everything out of your closet and actively choose what to put back, you will only put back about 55 to 60%—so you'll discard

40-45%. When Michaela and I looked at her calendar to decide what to cancel, she could barely bring herself to cancel anything. When she took everything off her calendar and had to choose what to put back in, she was better able to identify things that didn't add value.

To start the process of stopping the things that do not serve you well, print out your calendar for the next three days. Now, take a deep breath in, and delete everything on your calendar for the next three days. Exhale. Take a look at your printed calendar and analyze the necessity of each thing. Deliberately choose whether it deserves a place in your calendar. Once you do this a few times, you can start assessing how you can play with defaults so you're in charge of your calendar. Maybe you can change the default call or meeting time to 30 minutes instead of 60 minutes, so the assumption is that something should take 30 minutes unless an argument can be made to extend it to 60 minutes. Being in charge doesn't mean that your calendar will miraculously clear itself, but you will gain a sense of deliberate choice in what and who is going to take up your time.

Once you start asking yourself if you actively chose something that is in your life, you will start seeing the difference between quitting and stopping. I don't believe that it is ever quitting if you didn't choose it for yourself to begin with. And just because you chose something yesterday, that doesn't mean that you'll choose it again today. Every day is a new opportunity to choose what you want your life to be, so you get to say, *yeah, I chose that yesterday, but I don't want to choose it anymore.* If you are actively choosing something, don't quit when it gets hard to do. But, if you are not actively choosing something, stop doing it as soon as you realize that it has outlived its usefulness or that it no longer serves you well.

What I have found to be true in my own life and in the lives of many of the women I've coached through the years is that women are more likely to end up as the default doers for a lot of stuff in our personal and professional lives, especially the stuff that has to get done but gets no recognition or reward.

Jessie

Jessie is a tenured faculty member at a prestigious college. My team and I were working with the college on its inclusion and equity efforts, and Jessie was on the committee of six men and two women—all tenured faculty—that hired us. We were meeting with the committee weekly, and I noticed that Jessie took notes in every meeting, and she sent summaries of her notes around to everyone after each meeting. When I asked her about it, she shrugged and said that she had taken notes when they were initially interviewing consultants, and she had become the default notetaker for all meetings since then. I asked her if she enjoyed taking notes, and she said that she did, but she also acknowledged that it was exhausting her and preventing her from participating as much as she wanted in the meetings. I asked her if she would be willing to help me facilitate a portion of the next meeting, which would allow me to ask for a volunteer to be the notetaker for that meeting. She agreed and said that we should probably talk to the other woman on the committee, because she would probably be the first to volunteer.

At the beginning of the next meeting, I let everyone know that Jessie would be helping me facilitate the session that day, and that I needed a volunteer to take notes. First, everyone looked at Jessie. Then, all the men turned to look at the other female professor at the table. When the female professor did not volunteer, the men looked at each other with genuine confusion. One of them even voiced the confusion aloud—"Well, who is going to take notes, then?" We sat in silence for a few minutes before one of the other men spoke up and said, "I'm sure our department admin would be happy to do it. She can come up right away, I'm sure."

The administrative assistant did come to the meeting right away. She did take notes and send them around to everyone. Jessie asked her if she could support the rest of the committee's meetings, and she came to every subsequent meeting to take notes. Jessie was relieved, but she shared with me that she was very frustrated that it had only occurred to her colleague to enlist the support of an administrative assistant when neither woman had volunteered. "So, we were the admin support until we weren't, huh? That's terrible." Yes, it is terrible...but we can opt out of the mess by not volunteering or not volunteering again if we do it the first time. Let people know your default is a no unless you decide it's worth it to say yes.

Start taking charge of your energy by stopping what isn't necessary for you, what you didn't choose (and wouldn't have chosen if you had the choice), what exhausts you and adds no discernible value, and what you just plain don't want to do anymore. Think about the last week of your life. What did you "have" to do that irritated you, exhausted you, or stressed you out without adding any real discernible value to your life?

1. _____

_____

2. _____

_____

3. _____

_____

4. _____

_____

5. _____

_____

Now, pick one thing to stop doing. What do you have to do so you can stop doing that thing? Do you have to send someone an email, make a phone call, or just delete the thing from your calendar? Do that thing right now. Seriously, right now.

I trust you that you have done the thing you need to do to stop doing the thing you do not want to do. Scratch that thing off your list. Do you want to take any actions toward the other things on your list? The goal from now on to get (and stay!) in charge of your life is to find one thing every week that you stop doing. It will be difficult at first, but let me tell you, it will become one of the highlights of your week! The consistent practice of stopping the use of your energy to do something that is of no value to you is a profound practice of badassery!!

If you are having trouble getting yourself to stop doing a thing because you are plagued with "but it has to get done," the next section is for you!

Don't Do It, Get It Done

If you want to do a few small things right,
do them yourself.
If you want to do great things and make a big impact,
learn to delegate.
—John C. Maxwell

I have a very unhealthy relationship with laundry. I love fresh laundry, and I hate doing laundry. I cannot explain what I specifically hate about it. Each of the parts of doing laundry—gathering the clothes, sorting, washing, switching from washer to dryer, taking clothes out, folding the clothes, putting the clothes away—seems simple enough. I am even an excellent folder of clothes, I have been told. In college, I used to think it had something to do with the fact that the laundry room was difficult to get to in my dorm. In law school, I had a washer-dryer unit in my apartment, and I thought it was because law school was so hard. It didn't matter how much easier it became to do laundry; I was terrible at completing it.

So, why does seeing laundry in the hamper fill me with dread? Why do I force myself to start the process and predictably leave the clothes in the washer or dryer for days? Why do clothes from the dryer sit in the basket for days before they get folded and put away? Why do alarms and reminders go unnoticed when pertaining to laundry when my memory seems to work perfectly fine with everything else?

Many years ago, I was asking these questions aloud to my friend Marta, and she said something that changed my world. She told me that all those questions were the wrong questions to ask. She said that there was only one question I should be asking myself.

Why did I believe that I had to do the laundry?

What? I had to do the laundry because clothes got dirty and they needed to get cleaned, and I didn't want to wear dirty clothes. She listened calmly and said, *"I know that the laundry needs to get done, but why do you believe that you have to do the laundry?"* I immediately jumped into how I couldn't afford to have someone do my laundry. She asked me how much it was worth to me to never have to worry about laundry, if the laundry I put into the hamper miraculously got cleaned and ended up put away every week.

I don't remember what I said in return. I had probably fainted in pleasure at the thought. I was working on my Ph.D. at the time, and I was practicing law part-time. She took me through the process of calculating how much it would cost me to have someone come do my laundry every week, and it turned out that I would have to work a couple of extra hours a week to break even. That seemed like a tiny price to pay to make my laundry dread go away.

Still, I initially fought the idea. As a first-generation immigrant woman of color, I could not stomach the idea that someone else would come to my home and do my laundry. I voiced that concern to Marta, who was also a first-generation immigrant woman of color. She reminded me that as a first-generation immigrant woman of color, it was probably more important for me to excel at work and finish my dissertation. Well, when she put it like that, I quickly saw the wisdom in her words. Thank you, Marta!!

"I know that it needs to get done, but *why do you believe that you have to do it?"*

I have quoted Marta in dozens of coaching sessions with women who have tasks on their to-do lists that absolutely drain their energy and keep them from using that energy to get more important shit done, things like pursuing their goals, sleeping, hanging out with friends, taking a bath, doing nothing, or anything that reenergizes them. We need to start delegating or outsourcing these tasks. When I first bring this up, many women balk at the idea (just as I did) because of our deep socialization that there are tasks that we, as women, need to do to be good women, good mothers, good wives, good daughters, etc., etc., etc.

These tasks usually fall into three categories—"housework" (at home and at work), administrative tasks (like notetaking, organizing, scheduling, etc.), and emotional work (comforting, supporting, absorbing, etc.). After we read the Primal Scream series in the *New York Times*, about working mothers and COVID, my team and I decided to host "Women Scream!" Zoom sessions every Friday in March 2021 to honor women during Women's History Month. Dozens of women joined these calls—calls with no agenda or point other than to vent about what was frustrating them in their lives...the things that made them want to scream. Women vented. Women supported each other as they vented. Women cried as they talked about how much stress they were under, and women laughed hysterically as their vents took on the absurdity of what women actually experience on a daily basis, especially during the pandemic. I cannot possibly do the vents justice, so I'm including some of the vents shared in the chat during these scream sessions. These were responses to "what is something you really need to tell someone right now in order to feel a little better about all that you do?" (In order to make the sessions truly scream sessions, we required all chats to be in all caps!)

▷ I DON'T CARE WHAT YOU EAT, JUST MAKE A CHOICE.

▷ THE EDIT YOU THINK I MISSED WAS IN THE ORIGINAL DOCUMENT, I AM NOT AN IDIOT!!!!

▷ I CAN'T DO YOUR SHIT ANYMORE. DO YOUR OWN SHIT. PLEASE STOP GIVING ME YOUR SHIT TO DO.

▷ YOU TAKE THE NOTES! WHY IS IT ALWAYS ME?

▷ I'M JUST ASKING YOU TO BE RESPONSIBLE. NOTHING SPECIAL, JUST BE AN ADULT!

▷ I AM NOT BEING MEAN. I AM BEING DIRECT. GET OUT OF MY FACE IF YOU ARE GOING TO BE UPSET.

▷ NO. GO AWAY.

▷ WHY CAN'T YOU SCHEDULE THE SHIT YOURSELF?

▷ NO! I DON'T WANT TO HEAR ABOUT WHAT YOU ARE UPSET ABOUT.

▷ WHY ARE YOU IN CHARGE IF YOU ARE SO HELPLESS?

▷ WHY DO YOU THINK I CARE?

▷ I WANT TO HURT YOU.

▷ LEAVE ME THE FUCK ALONE. I DON'T KNOW.

▷ I MAY HURT YOU.

▷ AS SOON AS I'M ON A CALL, 2ND GRADE MATH BECOMES AN EMERGENCY. AND WHERE IS DAD? HMMM? HE'S ON A CALL. SO AM I!!!

▷ I DON'T WANT TO TAKE CARE OF YOU.

▷ CAN YOU EVEN SEE HOW MUCH SHIT I HAVE TO DO?

▷ I DON'T WANT TO DO THIS ANYMORE!

▷ WHY CAN'T THEY PUT ANYTHING *AWAY*???!?!!

▷ I CAN'T PICK UP AFTER MY HUSBAND AND MY TODDLER! WHY IS IT ALWAYS ME?

▷ FIX IT YOURSELF. OR GET USED TO IT BEING BROKEN.

▷ I CAN NEVER STOP AND SIT!!

▷ WHY AM I ALWAYS TIREDDDDDD?

▷ MY LIFE IS SO BUSY THAT ONE LITTLE THING GOING OVER ITS SCHEDULED TIME RUINS THE REST OF THE DAY UGGGGHHHHHHH!

As my colleague "rage read" these chats out loud, the women were laughing hysterically as they were listening and typing. As I sat back and watched the scene, it struck me how many of these things I have wanted to say and never said and how much energy it probably drained from me every time I swallowed the words that so desperately wanted to come out. As one of the rage sessions was closing, one of the women said, "You know what's really funny? When I read this list, I can't really tell if the woman is talking to a toddler, a teenager, a husband, a male colleague, or a male boss or all of the above? That really tells us a lot about why we need these scream sessions."

We will continue to do these scream sessions because so many women have reached out and asked for more opportunities to scream and vent with other women. We are equal parts grateful to play this role of convenor of screams, and heartbroken that so many women need to scream so much into just feel better for a little while. Let's keep screaming because it won't change overnight. And while we are screaming, let's also find ways to apply the "don't do it, get it done" strategy to get at least a couple of things that make us scream off our plate.

Pilar

Pilar is a brilliant scientist who leads one of the key research and development divisions of a pharmaceutical company. I don't use "brilliant" lightly: Pilar was the youngest person in her high school graduating class, skipped the undergraduate process by getting accepted into an undergraduate + Ph.D. combined program, and was speaking at national conferences about her research before she had even defended her dissertation. She also plays a leadership role in her company's women's initiative, runs marathons, and is the mother of 11-year-old twins.

I met Pilar when I was working with her company's women's initiative on gender differences in leadership styles and energy management, and she decided to try a few coaching sessions to help her "not feel like everything was rushed and on the brink of collapse all the time." When I asked her what she meant by that, she said that her life always felt like "it was one missed detail away from falling apart."

We started our work together by helping her identify what "collapse" and "falling apart" looked like. I asked her to close her eyes and describe to me what was happening in the complete disaster of full collapse. It took her a few minutes to get going, but then the fears tumbled out of her with such force that she talked for about 15 minutes without pausing.

"Kids get into trouble for always being late to school. They get to school on time but don't have anything they are supposed to have. They are the only ones who don't have permission slips signed for the field trip. They are the only ones whose mom can never chaperone a field trip. I miss an important email and miss a critical meeting. Everyone is talking about me behind my back about how disorganized I am. I can't get my blood pressure under control, and I end up having a heart attack, which I cannot afford to do right now. My husband leaves because I barely pay him any attention. I'm scared I won't even know if he's left because I'm so tired at home all the time. I hate cooking. I want to just order out all the time. That makes me a bad mom, doesn't it? Our garage is so messy that we can't park in there anymore. I am going to end up cursing at people on my team because they don't do anything I ask them to. If I were a man, they wouldn't go as slow as they are going. I don't want to be nice all the time. I am nice, but it's exhausting being nice all the time. I blank out when I'm driving, and I have to pull over sometimes to try and remember where I am and where I'm going. Maybe I am going crazy. What if I need to be institutionalized, not coached? Don't answer that. I used to be smart and organized. I have no idea where that person went. Why am I saying all this crap out loud? How is this even supposed to help me?"

Take a deep breath and read the excerpt of her "scream" out loud. Time yourself. All of that takes just about a minute to say out loud. One minute. She did this for fifteen minutes! She repeated a lot of things, got into deeply personal fears, including a long list of self-criticisms, and imagined some pretty terrifying scenarios, most of which were—in her fears—directly caused by something she did or did not do. Fifteen minutes after she started, she was breathing unevenly and sobbing and laughing all at the same time. She finished by saying, "I don't know what the hell the point of that was, but I feel better already. If this is what coaching is, sign me up!"

We talked about how women needed ongoing spaces where we can get out all of the worst-case scenarios that we are desperately trying to keep at bay so that we separate our fears of "everything falling apart" from problems that we may actually be able to solve, neutralize, or just consciously choose to ignore. And, then we began the process of identifying if any of the things on her to-do lists fell into the "get it done, don't do it" bucket.

We started with things on her daily to-do list, and she identified one that she dreaded to the point where she ruminated on it all day long: meal prep, everything from grocery shopping to planning meals to cooking. We then identified one weekly to-do that she despised—double-checking the lab entries at work on Fridays and getting everyone to correct anything they had missed all week so that she could sign off on them for the week.

I asked her how she could get these things done without doing them herself, and she immediately balked at the suggestion that she should get someone else to do these things. For many of the same reasons that I had resisted getting help with my laundry years ago, Pilar's hesitation was deeply rooted in what she felt she had to do as a mom, a caring leader, a hard worker, etc. To neutralize this hesitation, I asked Pilar to write down the cost of the time she spent doing these two activities that she really hated doing; her assignment was to think about the days that she went grocery shopping or put meals together or double-checked the lab entries and note where she was taking energy from to do these things.

When we surrender to the "I have to" because of whatever expectations we think we cannot disappoint, it is difficult to remember that we are taking the energy from somewhere else to meet these expectations. If we remind ourselves of what it costs us to meet these expectations, it is easier to see how "it needs to get done but I don't have to do it" can work in our best interest.

Being in charge is a dynamic process that you claim a little bit at a time. It isn't about fixing what you are doing; it's about paying attention to what is draining your energy and what is refueling your energy, then finding ways to minimize the former and maximize the latter.

Saying No

Exhaling requires stopping and subtracting. We've covered several ways that you can set boundaries within the universe of your responsibilities, but the most powerful tool in stopping and subtracting is to just say no. Don't accept things into your universe of responsibilities unless you actively choose them. Actively saying no is an essential tool in taking charge of our lives, but we most effectively learn how to use this tool once we learn how to set boundaries in the universe of what we have already said yes to. Setting boundaries for things that will stay in our lives is harder than saying no to new things, and when we are comfortable with the former, the latter becomes easier...and more fun!

Just say no.

If you want more time in your life to do the things you want to do, just say no. Easy, right? There was an article in USA Today in April 2021 with the headline "The One Word Women Need to Be Saying More Often."[14] The author of the article starts with the question "If you're a woman, when was the last time you said 'no' to a friend, your partner, a colleague of your kid?" The author continues "For many women, 'no' is a foreign word on the tongue." My stomach roiled when I read this. Yes, women need to say no to more things that end up in our lives even when we don't want them or choose them, but articles like this suggest that women just need to learn to utter this simple two-letter monosyllabic word.

There is a lot written about why women have a more difficult time saying no than men. The assertions are that women don't want to say no because we don't want to hurt other people's feelings, that we want to take care of people and do things for them, that we are socialized to want to please people. I call bullshit on this!

Women know how to say no. Watch a mother corral a toddler in a park, negotiate a curfew with a teenager, or stand up for her child with an ineffective teacher. Watch a woman direct a movie, represent a client in court, or ensure that her designs are executed impeccably. Women know how to say no. It's not a "foreign word on our tongues." But it is a word that we have often been hurt for uttering.

"No" is not a *foreign* word for women to utter. "No" is a *dangerous* word for women to utter. Saying no is easy for women when we know it is safe for us to do so. Saying no is difficult when we either know that it's dangerous for us to do or if we don't have enough evidence that it is safe to say. Saying no is not a simple choice that women can make; it is a calculation of risks and rewards, of costs and benefits, which requires extensive due diligence, careful experimentation, and clearly defined exit strategies in case things go wrong.

Yes, we need to say no more often, but we also need to recognize that most women who aren't saying no in certain situations have calculated that it is not in their best interest to say no, and we need to honor and respect that. It takes a lot of strength to want to say no, calculate that it will cost too much to do so, and bear the weight of putting up with something you really didn't want in your life. Not saying no is an act of courage just as saying no is an act of courage.

Being in charge of our lives doesn't mean that we suddenly find it easier to say no, but it does mean that we have to better understand why we don't say no when we really want to say no. Why was it easier to say no in one situation but not in another? Why was the risk calculus for saying no different with one person than with another? What data are we using to calculate the costs and benefits?

Saying no is not a binary choice we make in any particular situation. It's a process we undertake that has lots of moving bits and pieces, a process that requires experimentation, ongoing reassessment, and making peace with incremental progress toward a no.

∗ Leona ∗

Leona was a rising star in an accounting firm. Everyone she worked with gave her high praise on her work ethic, her attention to detail, and her sheer intellectual horsepower in solving difficult problems for clients. Leona's mentor told her how highly she was regarded by senior people at the firm and suggested that she work with one particular senior leader who had considerable influence in promotion decisions.

Leona approached this senior leader and was excited when he asked her to start working with him on a high-profile client matter. She enthusiastically jumped into the work and was soon seen as this senior leader's most trusted surrogate. Leona attended meetings and managed client calls on his behalf, and by all accounts, she was exceeding expectations and thriving.

Three months after Leona started working with this senior leader, he invited her to a meeting he was scheduled to attend with other senior leaders. He asked her to observe and take notes, and he told her that being able to see what happens in meetings like this is not something that many people her level was ever exposed to. She was grateful for the experience and excited to attend. When they walked into the meeting, the senior leader introduced her to the head of the firm and said with a laugh, "This is Leona. She is the best work wife anyone could ask for."

Leona cringed at his words, but she knew the opportunity she was being afforded to be introduced to these leaders and to be in this room, so she pushed aside her discomfort and moved forward to meet the next person. The "best work wife" comment was repeated several times, always followed by chuckles from the men, and with each recitation of the words, Leona became more uncomfortable. When the meeting was about to start, Leona went to the back of the room where other observers were sitting, and she realized that her head was pounding, and she was extremely nauseous.

Leona snuck in a strong dose of Advil and tried to listen to what was being discussed. She couldn't focus, and no matter how hard she tried, she couldn't find that enthusiasm that she had been brimming with just that morning.

After this meeting, the work wife comment consistently peppered any interactions she had with this senior leader. She talked to her mentor about how she felt when the senior leader kept referring to her in this way, and she asked her mentor how to ask this leader to stop calling her that. Her mentor's answer was short and swift, "Don't bring it up unless you want him as your enemy."

The comments continued. The work wife metaphor was used in various ways, ranging from "just like life, everyone needs a wife at work to keep things running smoothly" to "I dated a lot of people before settling down with Leona" to "Leona is something special, but she is taken." Leona's headaches came more frequently, and she realized that she was losing weight because she wasn't eating regularly. She had also not been working out because she had been working so much.

In one of our calls, she broke down and told me how many things this man said to her on a daily basis that irritated and upset her. "What is wrong with me? Why is it so hard for me to tell him to fuck off?"

"It's not hard for you to tell him to fuck off," I told her. "It's hard for you to deal with the consequences of telling him to fuck off." This is a distinction that makes a difference.

We talked through various things she could do to manage her energy in spite of this massive energy drain. She tried various things, but she couldn't shake the sense of feeling powerless.

Leona submitted her resignation just about six months after this leader first called her his work wife. She decided to take a break for a few weeks before looking for something new. She was and continues to be one of the smartest and strongest women I know, and it is her story that I remember whenever I hear anything about how women have difficulty saying no.

When I was in law school, a friend of mine and I were boarding a flight to Mexico to go on a vacation we had been planning for weeks. As we walked through the jetway to the plane, I noticed her getting paler and paler. By the time we were buckled into our seats, her face was ashen, and her hands were balled into tight fists. I asked her if she was scared of flying. She turned to me, her eyes wild and filled with a mixture of fear, desperation, and irritation. "I'm not scared of flying," she said through gritted teeth. "I'm scared of being high up in the sky and plummeting to the ground to my death."

The fear of flying, aerophobia, is a misnomer; it's actually a fear of what could go wrong when you fly. The fear of flying is actually a fear of crashing. While the probability of crashing is low, the naming of the fear accurately allows us to help people deal with what they are actually feeling.

Women are not afraid of saying no. We are afraid of what could go wrong when we say no.

Saying no is a journey women set off on, a journey in which they experiment with cause and effect and with costs and benefits without quite knowing what the experiment will yield.

ADD & AMEND

Being in charge is about feeling good. All of the tools in this book that allow you to be in charge are designed to help you figure out what makes you feel good, strategize how to do less of what doesn't make you feel good while you do more of what makes you feel good, and create processes in your life to make feeling good the natural default for you. Unfortunately, when women don't feel good, we try to add things to our life that do feel good—this is the ineffective bullshit woven into the ubiquitous messaging about self-care that is targeted at women.

When I'm exhausted and overwhelmed, there is nothing more annoying to me than reading an article on self-care that lists the hundred things I should do to feel better when I don't even have the energy to finish reading that article. It is important to add things into your life that feel good—but you can only add things after you first understand what gives you peace, joy, acknowledgment, and community, and also subtract all the things that do not belong in your life. If you add things into your life before you understand and subtract, the additions don't do you much good. It's why most self-care strategies feel good in the moment but don't have lasting effects.

Make Room for Good

Willa

Willa is an entrepreneur in the fashion industry. Soon after she launched her online design firm, one of Willa's projects was recognized for its outstanding design, and potential clients started calling with more work than she and her small team could manage. She was excited, but she also started worrying about whether the firm would be able to handle the work. She didn't know how to decide between potential projects, and she and her team soon found themselves working 12 to 15 hour days with no end in sight. They were enjoying their work, but they were rapidly getting burned out. "We are way too busy, but it beats the alternative," was an oft-repeated phrase in their team meetings.

As her team was visibly getting more tired with each day, Willa decided to integrate some wellness resources into the workplace. She hired a massage therapist to be in the office for six hours every Friday to do chair massages for anyone who wanted. Willa also hired a catering service to bring in healthy lunches and snacks every day. She received great feedback on the introduction of these resources.

A few weeks after she hired the massage therapist, the therapist told her that while people had signed up for the massages on the first Friday the service had been introduced, she had not been getting more than two or three people per day since then. Willa was surprised, but she knew that they were all very busy. She sent out a reminder message to everyone to utilize the massage resource to help negate the effects of working long hours every day.

Willa checked in with the catering service and received similar feedback: Although people were eating the snacks sporadically, people were not eating the freshly made hot lunches and salads the catering company was creating for them. She brought up these resources at their full team meeting and asked if people preferred that she discontinue the services since there didn't seem to be much interest.

People vehemently disagreed with discontinuing the services. "Every single one of them wanted me to keep the services. I don't get it. We were wasting money, but they didn't seem to want to not have the things they weren't using anyway."

I asked Willa how often she had signed up for the massages, and she sheepishly told me that she had yet to utilize the service. I asked her about the catered lunches, and she said that she had not often partaken of them. When I asked her why she hadn't used the wellness resources she herself had set up, she said that she was too busy.

I reminded her of the "one out, one in" principle. No matter how good the thing you want to add, if you don't take something out first, there is no space for it. Some expectation or responsibility needed to be removed in order for people to add in a massage or even a healthy catered lunch. Willa thought about this and realized that team leaders often scheduled meetings at the last minute and through the lunch hour. I asked her if the amount of time spent in meetings was a barrier to people getting their work done and if there was a way to block off time in the company's calendar where there were no meetings. Subtracting meetings and the expectation to always be free for meetings would allow people to add massages and healthy nutrition.

Willa ran this by her team and was surprised at the "giddy" response. "When I suggested less meetings, people got giddy with excitement. I asked why we were all meeting so much when no one clearly wanted that. I think we met a lot when we first started out, and that just became a habit. We needed to meet more often because we were trying to figure out how to get work. We've got work now. More than we can manage. We need to be doing it, not meeting about doing it."

Willa implemented "No Meeting Fridays." It became a day for people to get organized, get work done, and also get a massage. She also encouraged everyone to schedule meetings only between 11:00 a.m. and 3:00 p.m. whenever possible to give people time in the mornings and late afternoons to work independently. She also asked managers to order lunches for the whole group from the catering company whenever there was a lunch meeting.

As expected, the massage therapist was quite busy after that, and the catering company's work picked up as well. These were small fixes, but they were the exhales necessary to make room for people to inhale in new things.

Subtracting before adding is critical to breaking out of burnout to be and feel in charge. And subtracting and adding require you to know exactly what brings you peace, joy, acknowledgment, and community. You are experimenting with creating an awesome recipe for a life you are excited about leading. That life won't always be easy or comfortable, but it is one in which you get to choose the difficulties and discomforts you want to tolerate.

Amend Yesterday's Dreams for Today's Realities

*The woman I was yesterday
introduced me to the woman I am today;
which makes me very excited about meeting the women
I will become tomorrow.*
—*Shar,* Poetic Evolution

We often get stuck in past versions of ourselves—we are immersed in what used to interest us, personality traits that used to dominate, challenges we used to face, etc. Our interests change as our lives change, our personality traits evolve, we replace old challenges with new ones that mirror our growth. But when we are stuck in a past version of ourselves, we cater to that past version of ourselves while living in the present.

We are all constantly changing, and when we forget to update the ways in which we see and talk about ourselves, we end up trying to find peace, joy, acknowledgment, and community in a way that would have made a past version happy, but won't work for our present version. Being in charge of your life today requires that you give yourself permission to think, be, want, and do in accordance with the person you are today. And it may also mean forgiving yourself for thinking, being, wanting, and doing what you needed to in the past. As Maya Angelou said, *"I did then when I knew how to do. Now that I know better, I do better."* That can be true for every "today" of our lives in reference to yesterday and all the yesterdays before that.

You, Today

Inhale deeply through your nose. Exhale forcefully through your mouth. Repeat a couple of times to center yourself.

Take a piece of paper and divide the page into three columns. Label the columns "Past," "Present," and "Future." You can also use the chart below if you prefer.

Read each prompt below and reflect on how you would have answered the question in the past (it can be the recent past—as in yesterday—or the distant past...it's up to you), in the present, and in the future (it can be the immediate future—as in tomorrow—or a year or two ahead).

	Past	Present	Future
When excited, I...			
When sad, I...			
When happy, I...			
When angry, I...			
When hungry, I...			
When in the mood to socialize, I...			
On Friday nights, I usually...			
On Sunday mornings, I usually...			
After a long day, I...			
Before falling asleep, I...			
During the weekends, I...			
Success feels like...			
Failure feels like...			
Power feels like...			

	Past	Present	Future
Peace feels like…			
Joy feels like…			
Acknowledgment feels like…			
Community feels like…			

What has changed between the three columns? What hasn't changed? What did you feel as you pondered possible answers?

Now, remember one past version of yourself. Really picture the how, the when, the where, and other details about her. Imagine her giving you three pieces of advice. What would her advice be?

1._____

_____

2._____

_____

3._____

_____

She was a brilliant you, wasn't she?

Now, ground yourself in the present moment. Picture the future version of you exactly one year from today. Forecast the when, where, what she looks like, etc. What three pieces of advice do you want her to have from the present you?

1._____

_____

2._____

_____

3._____

_____

Take a few breaths and reflect on what you wrote above. What would you change about your present based on advice from your past self?

This is an exercise to help ground you in your own evolution through the passage of time. You are not who you were yesterday, and you do have a lot of control over who you will become in the future.

Opal

Opal painted murals in people's homes to put herself through art school. She had several shows of her work in small galleries, and she sold several paintings. She loved being an artist, but as a single mother, she couldn't rely on income from her art to support herself and her children. A friend of hers recommended her as an art consultant to his company's CEO so that she could try her hand in that field, and her career as an art consultant took off.

Within five years of that first art consulting job, Opal had her own firm with seven employees. She was nationally sought after as an art consultant for high-profile buildings in large cities, and she and her kids were thriving—physically, emotionally, and financially. They lived in a beautiful home that Opal helped design, and Opal was most excited that she had solid college tuition funds for both of her children.

During her oldest child's senior year of high school, Opal had a moment of crisis. She suddenly felt that she had sold out her original dreams of being an artist for material comforts. She wondered if she wasn't living her true purpose and if that was why she had so little interest in having a relationship.

Opal and I met in an art supply store, and when she started telling me her story, I asked her if I could interview her for this book. I met her at her house for the first interview, and I was awed by the design of the house and the landscaping as I drove up her driveway. The house was a beautiful stone and glass structure that seemed to blend in seamlessly into intricately arranged rock gardens. It felt like I was driving into a beautiful painting.

Given the carefully executed exterior aesthetics, I was surprised at how disorganized the interior was. It was clean and well-appointed, but several walls had been taped and prepped for painting, and there were cans of paint, magazines, paintbrushes, and other things strewn about on the floor and furniture. A few doors had doorknobs missing, and there were a few paintings propped against various walls. It looked like someone had not yet finished moving in, but Opal had told me that she had moved in more than three years ago.

Opal watched me take it all in and laughed. "This is what I'm talking about. This isn't who I am. I'm clearly not living my purpose and my space reflects that." She made us some tea, and I started by asking her what she meant about not living her purpose.

She told me that she was an artist at heart and that she had become an art consultant out of financial necessity. She enjoyed the work she did through her firm, and she loved working with her team, but she felt guilty most days because she wasn't painting more regularly. "When I moved into this house, I promised myself that I would paint murals on the walls, make my own doorknobs, create multimedia art for the walls and maybe even do some wood sculptures to bring the outside into the home." She looked around and shook her head. "It's been three years, and stuff just sits undone and messy. I had these dreams of entertaining friends in this house. My family and my closest friends come over, but they obviously overlook all this crap. It still makes me feel terrible that the house is like this."

I asked her where the kids hang out, and she told me that there is a separate entrance to the bottom floor for them, and the kids rarely came to this main floor. All of the bedrooms were one floor up, and she said while that floor wasn't a mess, but it was still bare of art and creative touches. The kids had done their own thing on the first floor with posters of movies and musicians. "They've just thrown up stuff as they felt like it. They've made it theirs, and I think they just put up with my excuses about this floor."

We talked about her work, her clients, and her team. We talked about her kids and her close relationship with them. She told me that she was close to her family, and she had friends that she loved and respected. She said that she had tried dating, but it hadn't really worked out. She was sure that once she reconnected with her passion for art that the relationship piece would fall into place. "I'm an artist at heart. I'm sure I'm supposed to be in a relationship with an artist and be part of a world filled with artists. Instead, I'm an art consultant. Twenty-year old me would have made so much fun of forty-year-old me."

We talked about a few other things in her life, and I asked her if I could contact her for a follow-up interview. She agreed, and I asked her if she would be open to trying an experiment. She was wary, but she cautiously agreed.

I asked her to write out everything she remembered about her twenty-year-old self—what that Opal liked, didn't like, wanted, was afraid of, hoped for, loved, was angry at, wished for, thought about, did, etc. I asked her to put that away, and the next day do the same ten-minute exercise for her forty-year-old self.

When we talked again a few days later, I asked her how she had felt after doing the exercise. She told me that her younger self felt too sugary, and her present self felt too salty. (I am always amazed at the metaphors that people come up with to explain self-reflections, but this was probably one of my favorite reflections ever!) When I asked her to tell me more about what she meant by that, she said that she had been too much of a dreamer when she was younger, and she wasn't enough of a dreamer as an adult. I asked her which of these selves wanted to paint the murals. "Oh, definitely the younger me wants to paint the murals. Ironic, right? Because the younger me wouldn't have been able to buy a home or design one like this one. Me today would have hired me from back then to come paint a mural for me."

Do you want to paint a mural on your walls, or do you want a mural painted on your walls, I asked her? Do you want to make unique doorknobs for your doors, or do you want unique doorknobs made for your doors? Do you want to create paintings and sculptures, or do you want paintings and sculptures created? She thought about it for a few moments and said that she didn't know. I asked her to think about it and let me know when she wanted to talk again.

She emailed me a few weeks later and attached a gorgeous picture of wildflowers growing on a hillside. "Can talk whenever you are able. Check out the picture. I'm mentoring a young artist who painted that for me. She is going to transfer that piece into a mural on my living room wall! Murals are a young people's game. I'm excited to support her and so happy to not be doing it." When we talked, she told me that she had decided that the murals and doorknobs were off her "to-do" list and were on her "get-done" list. With that off her plate, she was excited to create the wood sculptures, and she had already made inquiries about where to get the particular wood she wanted. "I made space in my garage to work on the sculptures. The painter is going to start on the mural in a couple of weeks, and it should take her a few weeks at most to finish. I'm going to have a mural on my wall by the end of this year!"

The peace and joy in her voice clearly came through when she was talking. "I don't think I want to be an artist trying to sell paintings to survive. I really like art consulting. I like making workspaces beautiful and meaningful through art. I like supporting talented artists. Maybe I was never supposed to be an artist."

I suggested that she was an artist. She was an artist and an art consultant and an architectural designer and landscape visionary and a sculptor and a lover of murals and a supporter of artists. She was all those things, and she was fully in charge of how much of each of those things took up space in her life at any given time. She had changed and evolved since she painted murals, and if she tried to live her life in the present based on what she had wanted twenty years ago, she couldn't enjoy all of who she was today.

Opal sent me pictures of her home a few months later. It was breathtakingly beautiful. She had a truly amazing eye for designing spaces. It was no wonder that she was a successful art consultant. She hadn't finished her sculptures yet, but she had funky new doorknobs made by an artist whose work she had purchased for one of her clients.

We don't like saying that we are abandoning our dreams, and we definitely don't like saying that we are choosing reality over dreams. Dreams are romantic and unblemished by what our lives actually need; reality, on the other hand, feels like what we are settling for after we have abandoned our dreams. These notions keep us stuck in our sweet dreams and discontent in our salty realities. It's as if there is an ideal version of our lives that exists in our dreams and a practical reality that we didn't create that feels like the ideal's exact opposite.

I propose that we can amend our dreams and amend our realities so that they get integrated into something that makes sense for our lives today. We don't have to abandon what our younger selves yearned for, but we need to recognize that the realization of those yearnings may not look exactly like we imagined. As with all things connected to being in charge of our lives, we will know what needs amending and what doesn't based on how we feel. If we don't feel good, we need to amend what we are doing no matter what we have told ourselves for however long about who we are or are not—and if we feel good, we don't need to change a thing.

Add a Little Wild to Your Life

Within every woman there is a wild and natural creature, a powerful force, filled with good instincts, passionate creativity, and ageless knowing.
—Clarissa Pinkola Estes

We weren't born distrusting and fearing ourselves. That was part of our taming. We were taught to believe that who we are in our natural state is bad and dangerous. They convinced us to be afraid of ourselves. So, we do not honor our own bodies, curiosity, hunger, judgment, experience, or ambition. Instead, we lock away our true selves. Women who are best at this disappearing act earn the highest praise: She is so selfless. Can you imagine? The epitome of womanhood is to lose one's self completely. That is the end goal of every patriarchal culture. Because a very effective way to control women is to convince women to control themselves.
—Glennon Doyle

Well-behaved women seldom make history.
—Laurel Thatcher Ulrich

You never get nothing by bein' an angel child
You'd better change your ways and get real wild
I'm gonna tell you something, I wouldn't tell you a lie
Wild women are the only kind that really get by
'Cause wild women don't worry,
wild women don't have the blues.
—*Ida Cox*

Whenever I get writer's block, I play music, and my "gotta find my real voice" playlist is an eclectic mix of women's voices that spans decades, musical styles, cultures, countries, languages, and ages. The array of differences between these women is vast, *but* the themes of their songs is achingly consistent—women can't win, or have much fun, if we play by the rules, and women who aren't afraid to break the rules get more done, have more fun, and change the whole damn system for the better for everyone.

These themes have begun to coalesce in the past few decades into messages of women remembering who we really are by shedding the selves we have had to adopt to survive and succeed in a world that wasn't created by or for us. These messages play with the idea of women connecting with our true selves, our wild selves, and they offer a path of taking charge of our lives by just not following the rules that have never worked for us. From Clarissa Pinkola Estes' groundbreaking *Women Who Run with the Wolves* to Cheryl Strayed's *Wild* (adapted into a blockbuster movie) to Glennon Doyle's successful *Untamed*, women's empowerment books have been adopting the notion of wild as free, uninhibited by society's expectations, and fun.

In the 1800s, the dancer Isadora Duncan advised women "You were wild once. Don't let them tame you." In 1924, Ida Cox, "The Uncrowned Queen of the Blues," crooned, "Wild women are the only kind that really get by/'Cause wild women don't worry, wild women don't have the blues." Natalie Cole sang "Wild women do, and they don't regret it/Wild women show/What they're goin' through/Wild women do/What you think they'll never/What you only dream about/Wild women do" in her 1990 hit song. In an episode of *Sex and the City* in 1999, Carrie Bradshaw noted that "Maybe some girls are not meant to be tamed. Maybe they are supposed to run wild until they find someone just as wild to run with." Your Smith, on the title song of her *Wild Wild Woman* album, sang about her inner wild woman: "I tried to leave her hiding, all strung up/I tried to keep her quiet, but she's screaming inside of me/I tried to keep her hiding, all shut up/I tried to keep her quiet/But she's a wild, wild woman."

This idea of connecting or reconnecting with your wild self can be interpreted in different ways by different women on different walks of life, but Glennon Doyle's words in *Untamed* sum it up in a universally applicable way: "I'm a grown-ass woman now, and I do what the fuck I want. I mean this with deep respect and love—and with the desire that you, too, will do what the fuck you want with your singular precious life."

What are some things in your life you want to do that you are holding yourself back from doing because it's not "appropriate," "proper," "wise," or whatever other word that has come to mean that you shouldn't do it? These are the things you want to do but you don't because of what someone else will say. This is not a theoretical exercise. Think of things where you can visualize the person/people whose criticism/whining/anger you are attempting to avoid. Visualize their reactions as you are doing the thing you really want to do. Visualize yourself continuing to do the thing you want to do even as the person/people are reacting in negative ways. How do you feel as you do this? What does it feel like to ignore their reaction?

No, pick one of those things you imagined and commit to doing it...today? Yes, today. Write it down.

In a recent workshop that I did for women on energy management, I asked each participant to write down a few things they really want to do but for whatever reason, felt they couldn't. They imagined the person/people, the reactions, and their feelings when they didn't respond to other people's reactions, just as you did above. Then they committed to selecting one of those things and doing that thing that day. These were some of the things they committed to doing the day after the workshop:

▷ I'm going to tell B no when he asks me to take notes on our call later today. He asks me because I say yes, and he depends on me to pay attention while he multitasks. I will tell him I can't today. If he pushes, I will tell him I'm driving.

▷ I'm going to go out to drinks with my friend tonight and tell my husband that he has to figure out dinner for himself and the kids tonight.

▷ I'm going to book the trip to Italy I've been putting off booking. I've been waiting for things to slow down at work. I'm going to book it and go regardless of what's happening at work.

▷ I'm going to start a job search for another job.

▷ I'm going to get my hair cut short like I've been wanting to for over a year.

▷ I'm going to break up with the guy I've been dating. I've been wanting to for a while and haven't because I didn't want to hurt his feelings.

▷ I'm not going to pick up the phone when my mom calls. She can complain about her life to my sister, her friends, or whoever else for a few days. I need a break.

▷ I'm going to play the music that I want to listen to loudly while I cook tonight. My boyfriend can watch whatever game he's watching on mute or he can go somewhere else to watch it.

▷ I'm going to find a concert I want to go to and buy tickets.

▷ I'm going to buy the red coat instead of the black one.

▷ I'm going to make pancakes for dinner.

▷ I'm going to go to bed at 10:30 no matter what is left in the house to do.

▷ I'm taking the painting of the horse down. He can put it in his office or anywhere else. I don't want it in my bedroom.

▷ I'm going to tell C that I don't want to be her bridesmaid. I don't know her that well, and I'm not even sure I want to go to her wedding.

These don't sound like wild things, right? But each of these was a "this is what I really want to do, but I will do something else to please someone else" thing in that woman's life that day. Adding a little wild in your life is about actively choosing yourself over someone else at least once a day. Of course, this isn't about shirking your responsibilities or doing something irresponsible. It's about accepting that someone will react negatively to your choice and doing it anyway, because you will survive the negative reaction. It may not be pleasant, but you will survive it. And every time you survive someone else's negative reaction to something you are choosing in your life; it will get a little easier to choose yourself and your needs and wants.

Adding a little wild into your life isn't about doing something flashy or crazy. It's about making decisions from the core of who you are. It's about choosing yourself over others. Just that one act of wild each day adds energy to that day. It's a reminder to yourself that you have wants and needs, and those wants and needs matter and require attention.

∗ Diana Rewilding ∗

I asked Diana in one of our conversations how the pursuit of being the "best high-riding bitch" was going. She explained to me that being a high-riding bitch meant being an arrogant, overbearing bitch, and that she was definitely getting better at it every day. "I've modified it, though. I'm a 'selective high-riding bitch' so you only see the bitch if you deserve to see the bitch."

Diana had done an amazing job of letting go and releasing and making space. "I've gotten very good at exhaling," she told me. "I just don't know what to inhale now." We talked about her discovering or rediscovering the untamed version of herself.

One of the things that I had discovered in coaching women is that our perceptions of ourselves are very different than the perceptions of people who love us and respect us. I asked Diana to write down all the words she would use to describe herself. I told her to then make a list of 10 people she trusted and ask each of them to come up with 10 words to describe her.

When we sat down to compare the lists, I could see Diana struggling to hold back her tears. I asked her what was making her cry. She told me that every single person had used the word "brave" and some version of "fighter/warrior." "My list had words like 'reliable' and 'honest' and 'hardworking.' My community had words like 'brave' and 'fighter' and 'fierce.' I want to be the person they are describing."

"You are the person they are describing," I told her. "You asked them to describe you, remember."

I told her to take out the list of words she had written about herself and tear up that piece of paper into small pieces. I asked her to go to the bathroom and flush those ripped pieces down the toilet. "Trust the people you trust. You asked them to describe you. They did. Let's go with what they said instead of what you think right now."

This exercise—and yes, flushing your list down the toilet or burning it is an essential part of the exercise—is a recalibration exercise. Diana selected a few words that consistently showed up on her people's lists, and she selected "brave," "fighter," "creative," "confident," and "leader" as her recalibration words.

The next part of the exercise was to ask herself the following questions every day?

▷ What does a _____ look like?

▷ What does a _____ sound like?

▷ What does a _____ do for fun?

▷ What does a _____ do to relax?

▷ What does a _____ read?

▷ What does a _____ watch?

These questions can vary based on whatever aspects of your life you want to focus on. They can include questions like:

▷ What does a _____ dream about?

▷ What does a _____ do when someone pisses them off?

▷ What does _____ want to see in this world?

The possibilities are endless!

Diana's homework was to complete a few of these questions for each recalibration word and act accordingly. This exercise is about releasing the patterns of behavior we have formed based on our sometimes-inaccurate perceptions of ourselves, and stepping into behaviors that align with the recalibration words.

Say the thing you must say.
Go where you must go.
Leave what you must leave.
Do what you must do.
Trust yourself.

When they say:
You seem out of control...
You say:
Thank you. That's the plan.
For the rest of my life.
— Glennon Doyle

CELEBRATE & CURSE

Did you know that celebrating and cursing have the same awesome physiological, cognitive, and emotional effects on you?[15,16] They both involve the deliberate or impromptu departure from the predictable and mundane to create a moment in time that makes us feel more connected to ourselves, our lives, and the world around us. Sometimes they make us laugh, sometimes they make us cry, sometimes they silence us in awe, sometimes they excite us with sheer silliness. But they always make us pause the pull of the future to reflect on the past and get grounded in the present.

When we celebrate anything at any time, the anticipation of the celebration and the joy in the celebration reduce stress levels, alleviate burnout symptoms, give our cognitive abilities a boost of energy, enhance our interpersonal connections, and generally make us more resilient when challenges and frustrations come our way. Similarly, when we curse at anything at any time, the venting of frustration or irritation reduces stress levels, alleviates, burnout symptoms, refreshes our cognitive abilities, and gives us a boost of pain tolerance that may be necessary to get beyond that struggle.

The above, of course, refers to the productive versions of celebrating and cursing because both have unproductive versions that aren't very helpful. When you regret—or don't even remember—something that occurred during the celebration, chances are that it was not productive celebrating. And, if you find yourself cursing at yourself or others to vent your anger or incite their anger, chances are that it's not going to end up being productive!

Productive celebrating is rooted in peace, joy, acknowledgment, and community—even on the most micro of scales. Productive cursing is the kind of cursing that you do when you stub your toe on a piece of furniture, or when you turn off your computer with a sigh and a curse because it's not doing anything it's supposed to do, or you curse at the television when your team misses a clutch shot to lose the game. I definitely do not advocate for any cursing of people (at least not to their faces!) or cursing as a way of avoiding facing or fixing a problem. But a well-timed expletive to release some frustration is not only productive, it can be quite fun as well.

Being in charge of your life isn't always easy, but if you integrate enough celebrating *and* cursing into each day in small ways, you will feel good regardless of what is going on around you.

The Science of Celebration

People of our time are losing the power of celebration.
Instead of celebrating, we seek to be amused or entertained.

*Celebration is an active state, an act of expressing
reverence or appreciation.
To be entertained is a passive state—it is to receive pleasure
afforded by an amusing act or a spectacle.... Celebration is a
confrontation, giving attention to the transcendent meaning
of one's actions.*
—*Rabbi Abraham Joshua Heschel*

What do you think of when you think of celebrations? Birthdays? Weddings? Graduations? Anniversaries? Holidays? Promotions? Reunions? The need to celebrate transitions in our lives is a deep human need that transcends time, geography, and culture. Historically, celebrations have been tied to cultural, religious, and social rites of passages, and to understand the deep human need to celebrate, it is useful to understand the role of rites of passage in our lives.

Rites of passage have been studied by anthropologists, psychologists, sociologists, and other social scientists for centuries, because these rituals tell us a lot about what is important to people and how people express that importance through individual and collective rituals. Rites of passage publicly and ritually mark the passage of time (birthdays, anniversaries, etc.), the change of status (weddings, coming of age, funerals, promotions, etc.), the achievement of something important (graduations, inductions into organizations, swearing-in ceremonies for public office, etc.), the reaffirmation of something important (pilgrimages, renewal of marriage vows, etc.), and the recognition of culturally/socially important holidays (independence days, religious holidays, days that honor people who have changed our world, etc.).

The public recognition and affirmation of the above, with ceremonies, festivities, food, music, dance, and community, refresh and energize us by disrupting our temporality (how we experience time) and spatiality (how we experience the space we are in).

TEMPORALITY: Think about how we measure the progression of time by our birthdays or how we divide up our years into chunks of time between holidays—after Thanksgiving, before Christmas, on Halloween, before Spring Break, after a birthday, starting on New Year's Day, etc. A celebration allows us to experience time differently by disrupting our usual patterns of experiencing time. Celebrating allows us to step away from our routines for a moment, to reset and refresh after a moment of joy and connection (with ourselves or with others). This temporal disruption through celebration is felt when we look forward to a vacation, a birthday celebration, or anything else that feels like it's a moment in time that is different than our usual routines.

SPATIALITY: Whether it is places of worship, a favorite bench in a park, the comfy chair in the family room, that particular beach at sunset, or anyplace that instantly transports you to that sense of peaceful joyful bliss, spatiality is that celebratory connection with a physical space. Being in the space is ritual enough, and even thinking about being in that space gives you a sense of comfort. While temporality is more intellectual, spatiality is more physical and sensual. While spatiality is often associated with the visual, certain smells, sounds, and other sensory experiences can evoke that same sense of celebration.

The psychology behind celebrations is essential to understanding phenomena such as burnout, chronic stress, and apathy. When we don't have enough celebratory temporal and spatial disruptions, our brains get worn out from the tedium of unvarying repetition. Breaking up the wearisome patterns revitalizes us; breaking up the wearisome patterns frequently keeps us revitalized, even in the most stressful of times and circumstances.

The big celebrations are built into our traditions and customs, but we can deliberately take charge of our lives on a daily or even hourly basis by creating micro-celebrations to break up how we experience time or to activate sensory experiences that evoke the positive emotions we want to feel regardless of what is going on around us.

Celebrate You in Time

"Life is what you celebrate. All of it. Even its end."
—Joanne Harris
Chocolat

∗ Sydney ∗

May 2020. Sydney had been recently promoted to an executive position in her organization, and she led a team of about 200 people spread across offices in three major cities. Her team had effectively transitioned to the sudden need to work remotely due to COVID-19, but Sydney had started to notice how utterly wiped out everyone seemed to be.

One of Sydney's friends referred her to the Wednesday Wellness Webinars that my firm had been doing since the beginning of the pandemic. These webinars were free to anyone who wanted to attend, and for one hour every Wednesday, people could tune in, practice simple mindfulness skills, and learn strategies to deal with the tragedy, chaos, fear, and confusion that all of us were absorbing during that time.

Sydney invited her team to participate, and several did, but Sydney felt like she needed to implement something more structured. She reached out to me to brainstorm ideas. I asked her to describe the kind of work her team did, and she told me that they were the facilities management hub for the parent company and several of their operating companies. She described the work as "consistently chaotic, consistently too much, and consistently never ending."

"This is an amazing team of people. They work their asses off, and they don't complain. They pitch in to help each other, and it's a big team, but you would be surprised how well people know each other. They really care about each other. I know the remote working is taking its toll, especially on the moms. We've increased access to our counseling services and other employee assistance programs. We have made some financial consultants available in case they need to rethink their spending and budgets. I feel like we are helping them deal with the big stuff, but I want to help with the day-to-day things too so that they aren't so exhausted."

She took me through what a usual day was like for a couple of people on her team, and it quickly became clear to me that for most people on this team, the workflow felt like water gushing from an open fire hydrant—a high-pressure push of a relentless volume of things to do. When I described this image to Sydney, she agreed and added, "It's also that when you start your day the water is gushing and you just jump in, and when you end your day, the water is still gushing, and the whole time you aren't working, the water is still gushing so it's hard to stop working because the water isn't going to ever really stop gushing."

I could only imagine how hard it was for her team to integrate mindfulness strategies when even their ability to eat and stretch their bodies was erratic. They collaborated and they did team huddles regularly, but they didn't really get together for meetings or trainings.

I told Sydney that I thought her team was being overwhelmed by perpetual stress, the kind of stress that has no beginning or ending or breaks even for a limited time. This kind of stress is different than acute stress—stress resulting from a dramatic event that is clearly defined—or chronic stress—stress that may have resulted from one or multiple recurring events that lead to prolonged and consistent stress, sometimes even after the events stop. With both acute and chronic stress, we focus on how to face it, go through it, stop it, or manage it in order to complete the stress cycle and move on. With perpetual stress, you can't complete the stress cycle; the situation has the stress built into it, and if it's a situation that we enter, the stress is unending until we exit the situation. Sometimes the answer is to never enter situations of perpetual stress, but sometimes we may engage in professional and personal activities that we enjoy that may be brimming with perpetual stress. In these situations, managing the perpetual stress can prevent it from becoming acute or chronic stress.

I gave Sydney (who was a recovering lawyer like me) the example of studying for the bar exam. From the day you start studying for the bar exam to the minute you finish the final question of the final day of the exam, you are in a state of perpetual stress. There is always more studying to be done. It's impossible to know when to start or stop studying because you can never know everything, and you don't know when you know enough.

The only way to manage perpetual stress—other than to exit the situation—is to segment the day and celebrate the completion of each segment. I asked Sydney to experiment with the concept in her life and then decide if it would help her team.

Celebrate to Destress

1. The first thing she needed to do was to make a list of things she absolutely enjoyed emotionally and sensually that took less than three minutes to do. (Figuring out what goes on this list is a dynamic work in progress, but if you'd like to try this, start with at least 10 things that you know for sure make you feel good from both sensory and emotional perspectives... and take less than three minutes to do.) Sydney and I brainstormed, and her list included:

   ▷ *Eat frozen red grapes*
   ▷ *Listen to "As" by Stevie Wonder and dance*
   ▷ *Do my back stretches*
   ▷ *Burn a candle and do a quick candle meditation*
   ▷ *Make and drink a cup of hot peppermint tea*
   ▷ *Write in my journal*
   ▷ *Text K to schedule next dinner/drinks/coffee*
   ▷ *Browse National Geographic's website to figure out next travel adventure*
   ▷ *Write a letter/card and send to S*
   ▷ *Schedule my next mani/pedi*
   ▷ *Do a body scan*

2. The second step was to go through the list of things she enjoyed and note what she needed on hand and ready in order to do the things on the list without much effort in the moment.

   ▷ *Eat frozen red grapes: need fresh washed grapes that are in the freezer in single-serving bags*

- ▷ *Listen to "As" by Stevie Wonder and dance: song queued on Spotify for easy access*

- ▷ *Do my back stretches: keep the lumbar pillow for the back stretch in easy reach*

- ▷ *Burn a candle and do a quick candle meditation: have a rose candle and a lighter ready and put the candle notes on a card by the candle*

- ▷ *Make and drink a cup of hot peppermint tea: make sure that peppermint tea is stocked, put water in electric kettle in morning to turn on quickly, and put a teabag in a cup ready for steeping*

- ▷ *Write in my journal: have the burgundy journal in easy reach, attach the silver pen to it*

- ▷ *Text K to schedule next dinner/drinks/coffee: no prep needed*

- ▷ *Browse National Geographic's website to figure out next travel adventure: have the travel page bookmarked and go directly to that page instead of tooling around with other articles*

- ▷ *Write a letter/card and send to S: keep addressed/ stamped envelopes with cards inside in easy reach*

- ▷ *Schedule my next mani/pedi: bookmark the appointments page for easy access*

- ▷ *Do a body scan: queue the quick body scan video on YouTube and bookmark the page so can just listen and do the body scan*

3. The third step was to scan the next three days on her calendar and divide her day into six segments. (If you assume a 16-hour day from waking to getting in the bed for the night, the 16 hours could be divided into eight segments of two-hour

blocks. But our days don't usually divide up that nicely, so six segments a day can mean that each segment is different, and each day's segmentation looks different from any other day's. The segments have to make sense. You can start with four or six, and you can have as many as you want, but you should definitely have at least four.) Sydney's segmented days looked like this:

Day 1

> ▷ *Segment 1: 6-9*
> ▷ *Segment 2: 9-11*
> ▷ *Segment 3: 11-4*
> ▷ *Segment 4: 4-10*

Day 2

> ▷ *Segment 1: 6-11*
> ▷ *Segment 2: 11-2*
> ▷ *Segment 3: 2-6*
> ▷ *Segment 4: 6-10*

Day 3

> ▷ *Segment 1: 6-8*
> ▷ *Segment 2: 8-1*
> ▷ *Segment 3: 1-5*
> ▷ *Segment 4: 5-10*

4. The fourth step was for her to note the segment end time in her calendar with a five-minute calendar entry. Then, she could either input the list of activities she had created into her calendar or write the list on an index card and keep it on her desk. The important things was that the list is handy when the segment ended.

5. The fifth step was for her to imagine what she would generally be doing during each segment and try to match a particular activity with a specific segment that seemed to pair with it. If so, she would note that in her calendar. If not, she would pick from the list based *on whatever struck her fancy in that moment.*

6. The sixth step was for her to brainstorm some celebratory phrases she could use to mark the end of each segment before she engaged in the activity. She was to add these phrases to her list so that she had the activities and the celebratory phrases handy in the same place. Below are a few she crafted:

   ▷ *Woo hoo! You rocked that segment!*
   ▷ *Cheers, girl!*
   ▷ *You kicked that segment's ass!*
   ▷ *Bye, Felicia.*
   ▷ *Yes, I am fabulous, thank you.*
   ▷ *Good thing I've been bullshit-proofed.*
   ▷ *That, ladies and gentlemen, is how it's done.*

7. The last step was for her to execute a phrase and an activity after every segment for the next three days.
   Sydney and I talked after the three-day experiment to debrief. She told me that she had not done every segment like she had planned but she had done at least four every day. She had even named her segments, and her list of celebratory phrases had doubled. She felt more in control over her day, and she felt like the segments had "gamified" her day. She was going to keep doing it.

   For her team, she decided to create six team-wide segments (four hours each over a 24-hour period, because her team worked-around-the clock shifts) with 10-minute "work free" breaks between segments. She asked her team to create more segments in their days as they needed, but these six segments became part of the managers' daily planning. Managers were able to check in on energy levels and productions by segments, which gave them more information on how people were organizing their workloads.

Just as birthday, anniversary, holiday, and New Year celebrations mark the passage of time by creating a pause in our routine experience of time, creating, and celebrating segments in our days gives us a temporal disruption that allows us to reset or refresh our attitudes and our objectives after each segment. Eventually, we become highly imaginative and skilled at creating powerful celebratory phrases and rejuvenating activities for segment transitions. In 2020 and 2021, there were several tough days when I had upward of 10 segments to help me get through the day!

Celebrate You in Space

Your sacred space is where you can find yourself
over and over again.
—Joseph Campbell

The bandstand is a sacred place.
—Wynton Marsalis, jazz legend

The kitchen is a sacred place.
—Marc Forgione, Iron Chef

A library is a focal point, a sacred place to a community;
and its sacredness is its accessibility, its publicness.
It's everybody's place.
— Ursula K. Le Guin, acclaimed author

Sacred spaces can be created in any environment.
— Christy Turlington

"Sacred space" is another way of saying "with intention."
— S. Kelley Harrell

Celebrating by disrupting our routine temporality is highly effective in adding peace, joy, acknowledgment, and community to our everyday lives. Celebrating by disrupting our routine spatiality is a different but equally effective way of adding peace, joy, acknowledgment, and community to our everyday lives. There is so much we can do by combining the power of these two types of celebrations, but let's dig a little deeper into spatial celebrations first.

Spatial celebrations are all around us in the form of sacred spaces, memorialized places, altars, and other spaces that are designated by individuals or communities to be places that mean something special, something out of the ordinary of how we normally use spaces. We have all types of buildings all around us, but places of worship are special buildings. People make pilgrimages to sacred places to reconnect with their spirituality. Spatial celebrations aren't just related to spirituality though; we celebrate spatially in any space that we consecrate as sacred to us.

In the quotes above, we see a legendary musician referring to the bandstand as sacred, a phenomenal chef referring to the kitchen as sacred, and an acclaimed author referring to a library as sacred. Artists refer to their studios as sacred spaces. teachers refer to their classrooms as sacred spaces. Joseph Campbell summarizes it most succinctly that "a sacred space is where you find yourself over and over again."

We women often find ourselves in circumstances at work, in our personal lives, or in larger society, where we are asked to be something other than ourselves, something less than who we really are. We are told that we can't be too smart, too strong, too beautiful, too powerful, too funny, too ambitious, too this or too that to be successful. We are also told just as frequently that we should be smarter, stronger, more beautiful, more powerful, funnier, more ambitious, and more and more to be successful. I don't know anyone that has ever been able to adequately explain what "just right" looks and feels like, but navigating the ups and downs of being too much or not enough is exhausting and drains us on a daily basis.

We have to create physical spaces in our lives where we are just enough, always enough, no matter what we look like, feel like, are like in that moment. Both temporality and spatiality are physically sensual and emotional experiences, and because of that, temporal and spatial celebrations are also physically sensual and emotional. Yoga studios and weightlifting gyms are both places where you go to move your body, but the spaces are designed to evoke vastly different physically sensual and emotional experiences. Similarly, our workplaces, our homes, the retail, and the hospitality places we frequent, etc. are all designed (intentionally or unintentionally) to evoke specific sensual and emotional experiences.

Intentionally engaging in a spatial celebration is a deliberate "visit" to a space that we have identified or created where we can be wholly, undeniably, unapologetically ourselves, even if it's for a just a few minutes every day. I purposefully use the word *visit* because part of the spatial celebration involves a departure from the routine space to deliberately visit the sacred space, then return to the routine space.

I've had people ask me if we can just make our routine spaces more sacred, and the answer is: hell yes, we can! If you can do that, go for it! The reality, unfortunately, is that most of us cannot escape the routine spaces that require us to get on the "too much/not enough" seesaw for big chunks of our days. Spatial celebrations are our ways to be in charge of our own energies, even if we are not in charge of how often we have to seesaw our way through the spaces in which we live our lives.

Is there a place that you have right now in your life where you go to just be, to breathe without worrying what you look or feel like, to tune out the world and tune in to yourself, to let the worries and frustrations fall off your shoulders for just a few minutes? When I've asked this question of women, I get answers ranging from "the nature preserves by my house" to "my bathroom" to "my car" to "the roof of my office building" to "the chapel at church" to "the coffee shop on the corner" to "my backyard" to "the art museum" to "the bench in the back of the park."

The place doesn't have to be fancy, but it does have to be easy to visit whenever you need it. Depending on the specifics of your life, you may need one sacred space at home, one at work, and one in between.

Self-Care as Celebration

Self-care is how you take your power back.
—Lalah Delia

True self-care is not bath salts and chocolate cake,
it's making the choice to build a life
you don't need to escape from.
—*Brianna Wiest*

The majority of what falls under the "self-care" umbrella, for women specifically, is rooted in the disruptions of our routines of temporality and spatiality through micro celebrations that allow us to reset and refresh our cognitive, emotional, and physical energies. But trying to figure out what self-care is increases stress more often than it reduces it. For example, a Google search for "self-care for women" results in more than 7 billion hits. Seven billion. Most of the women I've coached and those I interviewed on this topic shudder with anxiety at the thought of translating what these articles are saying into tangible and doable actions into their own lives. Where do you even start when there are 7 billion hits, and how the heck do you translate suggestions such as "recognize that self-care is not selfish," "be your own best friend," "believe that saying no is okay," or "prioritize yourself." And unless you regularly take yoga classes, get massages, or have a facial, how much will one session really change how much cognitive, emotional, or physical energy you have?

I often feel more exhausted after I try and figure out what to do for my exhaustion. I fantasize about clicking on an article on self-care that says something like: "If you need self-care, call 1-800-2RELAX, and we will take care of everything you need to do today so that you can take care of yourself. And no, you don't have to tell us what all those things are, because that would take forever and would not be restful, so we will magically figure it out, get it done, and send you a text when all is good." Fantasizing about that magical service relaxes me much more than researching self-care ideas!

Self-care strategies tend to fall into four general categories: 1) general physical and emotional health, 2) existing strategies for feeling good, 3) new strategies for feeling good, and 4) a system to keep feeling good. All the information on those 7 billion pages falls in line with these categories; but the lists of potential actions doesn't take into account how the four categories should be ordered or how they should be connected to each other. My observations, data gathering, and experiences suggest that there is a correct order, and if the actions from the different categories aren't connected deliberately and cohesively, a well-intentioned self-care strategy becomes yet one more item on our lists that adds to our frustrations and exhaustion.

1. General Physical and Emotional Health

This category is comprised of the activities that are necessary for our general physical health, including things like getting enough sleep, drinking enough water, eating healthy, exercising regularly, taking steps to decrease/stop addictions, getting massages, and maintaining an appropriate schedule of appointments with doctors, dentists, and other health care professionals. Activities to maintain our emotional health can include seeing a therapist; excising emotionally unhealthy people, behaviors, and circumstances from our lives; and maintaining the spiritual, familial, and personal connections necessary to make sure that we feel safe and stable in your life.

Many items in this category contribute to generally feeling good, but they are more directly related to paying attention to and caring for your body and mind in a practical way. The activities in this category tend to stay stable throughout our adult life even though we do add a lot of additional tactics as we get older, because there is just more to manage.

If the gears in this category are not whirring efficiently, it's difficult to feel good, even if you are consistent in scheduling and executing your leisure, creativity, and just plain fun activities. While those activities do buttress and enhance your physical and emotional health, those activities cannot substitute for your physical and emotional health.

2. Existing Strategies for Feeling Good

After, and only after, we have adequately executed on the activities we need to do to be physically and emotionally healthy, we should turn to what makes us feel good beyond the general sense of physical and emotional health that is the minimum necessary for being in charge of our lives.

This is where the suggestions for taking walks, baths, yoga classes, etc. come into play. If we already do any of these things, and if they make us feel good, we should prioritize them as they make sense. We can always add new activities to feel good, but we do need to start with what we already know works for us so that self-care doesn't become yet another thing on our to-do lists. Self-care should be the fuel that allows us to get to wherever we want to go; it cannot become another destination, another goal for us to achieve.

In the table below, write down five things below that you currently do that make you feel good—these should be the things that fuel you. Don't write down things that your ideal you wants to do or thinks you should do. Only include things you already do right now, even if you don't do them as consistently as you would like. Take a few minutes to reflect on and note the circumstances that make it most likely for you to do these things as well as what often prevents you from doing these things. Examples from women who have completed this chart include:

▷ Going for a run in the morning...happens when I get ready for my day the night before and I get at least five hours of sleep...doesn't happen when I forget to block my calendar to avoid last-minute scheduling or if I'm traveling or if I had too many drinks the night before...

▷ Uninterrupted and unrushed bath time in the evenings with the twins...happens when I don't check my phone during that time and if I put a phony call on my calendar so people think I'm busy...if I get home too late or if I get home and don't change into my sweatpants right away or I haven't eaten lunch because I'm too hungry then...

▷ Dinner and drinks with my sister...on weekends because of work for me and for her because her husband is at home to help with kids...doesn't work when we schedule on weekdays, brunch on Sunday mornings doesn't work...

▷ Yoga...ugh, trying to do hot yoga only makes me avoid yoga because it takes too much time to do my hair afterward...I don't miss yoga when I do the relaxing yoga classes or the yoga/meditation classes...

▷ Baking breads and cookies...any day works if I have the ingredients and it really works when I know I'm going to give the stuff as a gift...

▷ Taking a long bath and listening to music...do it when I plan for it, do it on days when I finish a project or meet a deadline...I put off running the bath and then it's too late, and I don't plan for it...

As the examples above illustrate, these aren't fancy or complex things. They are the things you do on a regular basis that you look forward to, things that break up your day and refuel you.

Doing this makes me feel good…	I am most likely to do this on these days and/or in these circumstances…	What keeps me from doing this as often as I want to is…

Do not continue reading if you haven't listed at least a couple of things. You can add more activities later. Now, before you continue reading, mark on your calendar the next time you are going to do one of the things you listed.

3. New Strategies for Feeling Good

We should always be looking out for new ways to feel good; in fact, trying new things is a self-care strategy in and of itself. That said, we should look for new things to try after we have identified what already works for us and made sure that we are integrating what already works solidly into our lives. Here are a few ways to discover and try new strategies for self-care…without overwhelming yourself.

▷ Keep a running list (in a journal, on your phone, etc.) of things you see, hear about, or read that pique your interest. Experiment with trying one thing on that list every month.

▷ Ask your community what they do for self-care. Experiment with creating a self-care date with friends, family, or others in your community.

189

▷ Identify when you need to refuel the most to discover what kind of self-care will best refuel you. Experiment with self-care activities that take less than 10 minutes to refuel in the middle of particularly energy draining things in your life.

4. A System to Keep Feeling Good

Self-care should ideally be an automatic system of physical, emotional, and cognitive celebration habits that are baked into your life. The habits are celebrative because they break up your day, the patterns that keep you stuck. This can sound counterintuitive because you're considering using patterns to break up patterns. But it's not the patterns that are the problems; it's where the patterns come from. Self-care is a system of patterns *you* create that are 100% *your* choice, things that make you feel unequivocally good, things that give you energy every time. This system of patterns helps you disrupt patterns that you are engaged in every day that you don't have much/any choice in, things that don't allow you to be completely yourself or give you the peace, joy, acknowledgment, and community that recharges you from the inside out.

For example, if you have to commute for an hour every morning to work, that commute may not give you peace, joy, acknowledgment, or community. But you do have control over what you do during that hour—as long as it's safe to do while driving. You can start by asking yourself how you feel when you arrive at work—if you feel peaceful and joyful and great, don't change a thing. But, if you feel tired, anxious, or bad, ask yourself what you did during the drive—did you listen to the news, did you take a call, were you comfortable in your car, etc. If you usually listen to the news, listen to music instead and see if you feel better. If you usually take a work call, see if you can avoid that or schedule a work call that you will enjoy instead. If you are uncomfortable because your back hurts, invest in a lumbar pillow. If your car is messy, and that bothers you, take two minutes to clean it out the night before. By disrupting the experience of the commute by listening to music that you can sing out loud to, it becomes a celebration. Is it anything other than a celebration if you are singing Adele or Prince or Beyoncé? Is it anything other than a celebration to listen to an entire album from your teenage years or an entire symphony or a really irreverent comedian? We often find ourselves filling our time with more ways to be better—self-improvement, learning a new language, etc.—and that's great if it brings you joy, but sometimes the best way to work on yourself is to do stuff that makes you feel good.

The system should work in a way where our self-care habits become as organically automatic in our lives as brushing our teeth and showering. I'm not suggesting that there is a perfect system that works for everyone, but I have seen some things that consistently work.

▷ Identify the self-care activities that you want to habituate. Write them down and then use reminder tools such as your calendar, your to-do list, habit apps, etc. to keep these actions in front of you so that they can become habits.

▷ Use "habit stacking" to more easily integrate new activities into your life. Connect new activities to established habits so that the new pattern you want to create leverages the existing pattern. For example, I realized I needed to drink more water during the day, and just reminding myself to drink water didn't cut it. So, I habit-stacked drinking water to conference calls/webinars (which I have in plenty every single day). I would start my workday with four bottles of water on my desk, and I would drink water after every call/webinar. Every time I hung up the phone, clicked off

Zoom, or disconnected from a live person during the day, I would drink water. Pretty soon, the four bottles would be empty by around 2:30pm. I eventually automated getting water through Amazon because I was running out of water. Self-care of hydration habituated.

▷ Create accountability mechanisms to hold your feet to the fire on transforming self-care into automatic habits. Is there someone in your community who wants/needs to work on the same habits as you? Can you partner up to hold each other accountable? Is there someone in your community who would just be good at holding you accountable? I have a barter system with one of my friends—she holds me accountable, and I buy her drinks. Whatever works!

▷ Schedule time off—between meetings, or one Friday a month, or a mini vacation,or anything that breaks up the routines you cannot control. Look at the month ahead and schedule time off. Do it again for the quarter ahead and the year ahead. Build in your moments of celebration as far in advance as you can. You can figure out how to celebrate later...first, make the space for the celebration to occur.

▷ KISS it. KISS is the acronym created by the US Navy in 1960 that stands for "Keep it simple, stupid." It's not the nicest way to talk to someone (especially yourself), I know, but the idea of keeping things simple is very powerful in creating any system that will work. I think of KISS as "keep it short and simple." Anything that is short and simple has a higher probability of getting done and staying in place than something that isn't short and/or simple.

What a Wonderful World
Louis Armstrong

I see trees of green
Red roses too
I see them bloom
For me and you
And I think to myself
What a wonderful world

I see skies of blue
And clouds of white
The bright blessed day
The dark sacred night
And I think to myself
What a wonderful world

The colors of the rainbow
So pretty in the sky
Are also on the faces
Of people going by
I see friends shaking hands
Saying how do you do
They're really saying
I love you.

The Science of Cursing

A wise woman once said "fuck this shit"
and she lived happily ever after.
—Anonymous
(pretty sure it's a woman)

* Washoe *

In the 1960s, psychologists Allen and Beatrix Gardner from the University of Nevada at Reno adopted Washoe, a West African chimpanzee, and raised her as much like a human child as they could. Washoe, named for Washoe County, Nevada, had her own living space with a bed, a couch, a refrigerator, and a living room. She had clothes, toys, and books, and she went on drives and ate dinner with the Gardners. She was taught American Sign Language (ASL) as her primary language, and the Gardners and other researchers who worked with Washoe only communicated with her and with each other in her presence in ASL, a strategy designed to mimic how human children learned language.

When she turned five, Washoe was adopted by Roger and Deborah Fouts, researchers at University of Oklahoma's Institute of Primate Studies. The researchers wanted to see how Washoe would use ASL when integrated into a community of other chimpanzees and if she would be able to teach them ASL in addition to continuing to build her own vocabulary.

Washoe ended up learning over 350 words. She used ASL to communicate complex thoughts and emotions with the researchers. Washoe had babies and taught her babies as well as other chimpanzees in the community to sign. By watching how the chimpanzees used ASL, taught each other new words, and communicated with each other and the researchers, the researchers were able to understand how much the community of chimpanzees looked and acted like a community of humans.

The following story illustrates just how sophisticated Washoe was in her ability to express her emotions and even her empathy for others. Washoe didn't like people to ignore her, so if someone didn't come to see her for a few days, she would frown at them and not "talk" to them. Roger Fouts recalled a time when Washoe was purposefully ignoring one of the researchers, Kat, who hadn't been around for a few days. Kat, in ASL, apologized to Washoe and decided to tell her—one mother to another—why she had not been around. "My baby died," Kat signed to Washoe. Fouts recalls that "Washoe stared at her [Kat], then looked down. She finally peered into Kat's eyes again and carefully signed "CRY," touching her cheek and drawing her finger down the path a tear would make on a human [because] chimpanzees don't shed tears [in the same way].[17]

Researchers were expecting Washoe to teach us how similar chimpanzees and humans were in how they learned and used language to express emotions. Washoe did that brilliantly, but what researchers did not expect Washoe to do was start cursing.

Early in her ASL lessons, Washoe learned how to sign the word "DIRTY" to indicate poop or shit. She used it to describe her feces or items soiled by her feces. A few years after Washoe learned this word, she became angry with Debbi Fouts because Debbi cleared the lab of people to record the chimpanzees' interactions when humans weren't around. Later, when Debbie watched the tape, she saw that Washoe had positioned herself in front of the camera after Debbi had left the lab and signed "DEB DIRTY." When one of Washoe's sons made her angry by stealing one of her magazines, she signed "DIRTY DIRTY" when she figured out what had happened.[18]

Researchers who study chimpanzee behavior note that when chimpanzees get angry with each other, they often throw excrement at the offending chimpanzee. What Washoe had figured out how to do through ASL was to metaphorically throw shit at offending parties without getting her hands dirty, so to speak.

Cursing is an effective way to express and release negative emotions in a way that is highly beneficial in the short term—it's far cleaner and faster to call someone a shit than to gather up feces to fling at them, and it's far more psychologically healthy than not calling someone a shit or flinging feces at them.

If you don't curse, don't think it's a good idea to curse, don't like people cursing, or just don't give a shit about the topic of cursing, please feel free to skip ahead to the next section. But, before you do, please know that reliable, defensible science has demonstrated that cursing when we are hurt can help us better tolerate the pain, and that cursing when we are upset can build emotional resilience and help us cope when we can't control what's happening around us.[19] Cursing can also be a form of creative expression and help us stay connected and relaxed. I'm guessing that the last point has to be qualified—cursing can help us stay connected and relaxed… around other people who curse.

I'm not arguing that anyone who doesn't curse should take up cursing (unless they really want to!); I'm just saying that when people do shit that makes them worthy of having shit thrown at them, it's better to just say *shit* than throw shit at them. And either of those choices, in my opinion, is better than letting them get away with that shit.

If this is still not your cup of tea, I completely understand. Please feel free to jump ahead to The Power of Anticipation and Celebration.

Curse It!
The Not-So-Subtle Art
of Saying Fuck It

When angry, count to four.
When very angry, swear.
—Mark Twain

Swearing is an art form. You can express yourself
much more exactly, much more succinctly,
with properly used curse words.
—Coleman Young

If you are still reading this, I'm assuming that you are good with cursing or are at least curious about exploring cursing as an energy management strategy, so let's fucking get on with it, shall we?

I didn't always curse as much as I do now. I was never opposed to it per se, but I realized that it was a way to channel my frustrations when I was in law school. Maybe I was around a lot of people who cursed or maybe it was always in me, and the stress of law school activated my ability to use the full extent of my vocabulary. I just know that one day I was in my Constitutional Law class, engaged in a debate with a classmate about the Fourteenth Amendment and affirmative action when he turned to me and said, "Of course, you would be in favor of affirmative action. You wouldn't be here if it weren't for affirmative action."

Lots of words went through my head in that moment—big words, fancy words, legal words, persuasive words. What came out of my mouth was, "What the fuck are you even talking about?" He looked at me in shock and said, "There's no need for profanity." I replied with "I agree. I didn't need to curse at you. I just wanted to." I'm sure I cursed countless times prior to that day, but since that day, I have cursed with more self-awareness, greater accuracy, and more thoughtful deliberation.

Profanity is generally defined as offensive or obscene language, and what I find interesting is that my classmate's racist statement wasn't considered profanity, but my question to him was. I don't agree with the notion that people curse because they don't have a fuller vocabulary; I think curse words make my otherwise quite extensive vocabulary even fuller.

Finley Peter Dunne, a Chicago humorist, captured my take on cursing when he said, "Swearing was invented as a compromise between running away and fighting." Washoe, the wise chimpanzee, understood this. When the researcher pissed off Washoe, Washoe didn't want to fight, but she didn't want to run away. So, she cursed at her in ASL. There are too many situations that women find themselves in when we won't win if we fight back but we won't forgive ourselves if we run away. So, we stay and curse.

I have not found better or more succinct ways to say, "Fuck it!" or "Bullshit!" or "What an ass!" or just "Shit." I have definitely not found ways to express those thoughts in ways that make me feel like I've released a bunch of negative energy that wasn't mine to carry.

Fuck it! Curse when you need to—or curse just because you want to. Curse not because it will do some good, but because it feels good. If you think it's just your imagination, it's not: Science has your back. Your body actually feels better after you curse. Your mind feels less stressed. Your emotions feel a bit cleansed. And those people that tell you to stop cursing because it's offensive? They are exactly the people for whom curse words were created.

*In my life, I have given a fuck about many people
and many things.
I have also not given a fuck about many people
and many things.
And like the road not taken,
it was the fucks not given that made all the difference.*
—*Mark Manson*

∗ Kai's 'No Fucking Way?!' Strategy ∗

Kai first uttered the words "no fucking way" in a team meeting because she had lost a bet with one of her teammates. The loser of the bet had to say "no fucking way" in a team meeting and act completely normal during and after saying it. Kai was terrified; she was the conservative, dependable person on the team. She just knew that her other teammates, mostly men, would ridicule her endlessly after she said it.

The meeting was almost over, and she had to say it before the meeting ended, so when one of her teammates looked at her and asked if she could be responsible for pulling together the materials for the upcoming training, she blurted out, "No fucking way." Her teammate was surprised by her response, and he immediately said, "I know it's not technically your job, but you always do it." Kai repeated, a little softer this time, "No fucking way." He told her that he would handle it, and that she didn't need to be mean about it.

She had every intention of apologizing to him later, but as the day went on and she didn't hear from him about the training materials, she wondered if she had stumbled onto something.

She and the two other women on the team were constantly asked to do things that none of her male teammates wanted to do. The assignments would be prefaced with "Can you help me out with something?" or "I really need a favor" or "I would so appreciate if you could do this for me." Whenever she tried to say no, she was told that she really needed to be a team player. During one particularly busy month, she had insisted that she couldn't do something for someone, and her team lead had called her to remind her that being a team player was one of the core skills that everyone was evaluated on for promotion and compensation.

But, whenever she had asked for help on something, no one seemed to have time to be a team player and help her. When she went to her team lead, she was told that people were really busy, and she really needed to be more independent and resourceful in getting her work done. So, she needed to be a team player and say yes when other people asked her for help, and she needed to be a team player and understand when other people told her no when she needed help.

The day she said "no fucking way" to a request was the first time that a "no" was treated like a "no" without any whining or follow up from the team lead. She was not someone who cursed at work, so the idea of saying "no fucking way" felt discomfiting. At the same time, not having to do the extra work—work that she didn't have the time to do and wouldn't get credit for doing—felt quite good.

She tried it out a few more times in meetings, and it continued to be effective. She anxiously awaited the call from her team lead that she was sure would happen, but that call never came. She became so concerned about the lack of this call that she scheduled a one-on-one to check in with him about how she was doing and what she needed to focus on to grow. He told her that she was doing well, and he gave her a few suggestions for growth projects. He told her that there would be several promotion opportunities in a few months, and he was confident of her ability to be competitive for the promotions.

She left that meeting somewhat confused; she had been sure that he was going to say something to her about her cursing. Given the positive tone of that meeting, though, she decided to continue to experiment with her "no fucking way" strategy. Every once in a while, she would catch herself saying it as a question instead of as an assertive answer, but no matter how she said it, it seemed to work better than anything else she had tried in setting boundaries.

When Kai first told me this story, she immediately asked me to not include it in the book. I asked her why she wouldn't want me to include it, and she said she just didn't want to come across like she was the type of person that cursed so deliberately at work. I asked her if she was still doing it at work. She laughed and said, "Fuck yes, I am." Then, she said, "Fine, use the story."

REST, RECHARGE, RESET & RESTART

Tech Reminds Us of What We Already Know

Have you ever checked out the power and battery settings on your laptop or your smartphone? Not only are the settings quite extensive and detailed, but they also make it look like our laptops and phones are self-aware machines that know themselves so well that they can communicate with us, telling us about the relationship between what we do for them and what they do for us.

First, they are very effective at telling us just how much charge they have left, and they warn us when their charges are low that they will turn off if we don't provide them with more energy. They also let us choose what to do when they are plugged in and charging, and what to do when they are running on battery power.

They tell us how we are draining their power and how much longer we can continue doing that before they will shut down. They don't care if we are almost done typing that text or if we were trying to finish just one more sentence before saving that document: They will turn off when the battery is drained regardless of what we have left to do. They warned us, after all. They have different modes they can engage to best use the charge they have, and one of the modes is a sleep mode!

Charging our tech tools has become a ubiquitous metaphor for charging our own energies. The metaphor lends itself to some pithy aphorisms about battery levels, draining and replenishing our energy levels, and plugging into the right recharging resources. The metaphors are useful, but they miss the larger lesson about the language surrounding our tech.

We humans created the language for technology battery and power usage, and we are now borrowing that same language to think about our lives. *We aren't learning from our technology; we taught these terms to technology based on what we know about how we humans work.* We use the word *crash* to describe what happens to us when we overload ourselves, and we gave that same word to our tech gadgets to describe what happens to them when they're overloaded. When we run out of juice, we have to go to sleep, and we gave technology a sleep mode for when it starts running out of power. We talked about "being charged up and ready to go" before we invented any technology that needed to be charged up.

It's fascinating that we use technology charging metaphors as if they came into existence independently of us and have something to teach us. We already know these things. We have always known them. We don't need the language of technology to teach us how to think about our energy levels, but we do need to look at how we treat our technology to question why we treat our technology better than we treat our own bodies and minds.

Our bodies and minds and our technology use the same language around energy, but we face four general challenges that make it easier for us to listen to our technology but rather than our bodies and minds. When we better understand and actively start neutralizing these challenges, it becomes easier for us to listen to our bodies and minds.

1. We don't have accurate battery icons like our technology that tell us exactly how much energy we have left.

2. We have subjective (awful!) judgements about ourselves and others when our batteries have a low charge. As a result, we focus on telling ourselves and others to try harder instead of looking for a charger and an outlet to plug into.

3. We don't know how to prioritize what we do based on how much energy we have, so instead of stopping the energy drains, we burn out.

4. We have not really examined how we recharge and what we need to recharge, so we keep going until our batteries die, instead of knowing what our chargers look like and which outlets we need to plug them into.

REST
Go the F*ck to Sleep

Rest is not idle, is not wasteful.
Sometimes, rest is the most productive thing you can do
for your body and soul.
—*Erica Layne*

Where there is a lack of rest, there is an abundance of stress.
—*Lysa Terkeurst*

I confess that I was one of those people who frequently said, "I will rest when I die," until one of my dearest friends, a devotee of getting at least eight hours of sleep every night, said to me, "You know the guy you are quoting kind of took it back and died at 56, right?" No, I had not known that. I hope he is resting in peace, and okay, maybe, that's not the best approach to the idea of rest.

When my kids were infants and toddlers, it was inescapably evident when they needed to go to sleep and just as evident if they had not had enough sleep. It was as if they had battery icons built into their minds and bodies. As soon as the battery was low, they would start getting cranky, rubbing their eyes, pitching dramatic tantrums, and, ironically, refusing to take a nap. Infants and toddlers respond automatically to these inner energy signals, but as they get older, we adults teach them to ignore these signals just as we have mastered the art of ignoring them.

Parents are the first witnesses to children learning the skills of ignoring their energy signals and doing whatever it takes to avoid sleep. The book *Go the F*ck to Sleep,* by Adam Mansbach, is a painfully prescient and humorous take on a parent trying to get a child to go to sleep at night. When I first read it, I laughed out loud at the similarity in antics engaged by kids to avoid sleep, and I cried in empathy as I remembered my own nights of living through those enterprising antics. The book has resonated so strongly with parents that there are now dramatic readings of the work by actors like Samuel L. Jackson and Jennifer Garner available on YouTube.

As I've read the work over the years, it occurred to me that the book is perhaps for adults to read to themselves about themselves. Take a few seconds to read and reflect on the excerpt from the work below:

"The cubs and the lions are snoring (snore)
Wrapped in a big, snuggly heap.
How come you can do all this other great shit
But you can't lie the fuck down and sleep?"

How come you can do all this other great shit but you can't lie the fuck down and sleep? Think back on the last week. How many nights in the last week did you go to sleep later than you wanted to, needed to, or intended to? How many nights would the above line from *Go the F*ck to Sleep* been applicable to you? For me, the line is probably applicable most nights of any week (regardless of when you are reading this.)

As adults, we are passionate about our children getting the sleep they need because we know that sleep is critical to their physical, cognitive, and emotional health and happiness. When did we forget—or refuse to remember—that sleep is equally critical to our physical, cognitive, and emotional health and happiness?

Rest is not optional; it's a necessity. If we do not honor and meet that necessity, it is difficult for us to take charge of our lives. It is difficult for us to create, find, and feel the peace, joy, acknowledgment, and community that comprise the bedrock of being in charge of our lives. The urgency to prioritize rest is being shouted from the rooftops, and when we hear the message, we nod as if to say "of course, I agree, 100% with that." But that agreement doesn't seem to be translate into us actually getting more rest.

If you are even just a little like the women whose stories are in this book, you probably agree wholeheartedly with the call to get more rest, but this agreement comes with several questions and thoughts that you don't quite know how to process or answer. The following is a compilation of questions and thoughts that women said go through their heads when they tell themselves to get some rest:

> *I need a nap, but I don't need what waits for me on the other side of the nap if I don't do this stuff.*
>
> *If I don't do the laundry, the kids won't have fresh clothes for school, and how do I deal with that? What about making their lunches?*
>
> *Who will check to see if everything is ready for the meeting tomorrow? I can assign that stuff to someone, but I will still pay the price if it's not ready, right?*
>
> *Can I really put off paying the bills one more day? Won't it actually be more peaceful if I get some of these things done and get less sleep?*
>
> *I probably won't be able to sleep if these things aren't done anyway. It's not that I don't want to sleep, it's just that now is the only time I can peacefully do all the things on my list.*
>
> *If I don't get a head start on this document tonight, I will pay the price tomorrow.*
>
> *I have to talk to my sister because I was too busy to talk to her all day. I don't not want to sleep.*

I just feel numb right now. If I had a couple of drinks, I would be better able to slow down my thoughts so I can sleep.

How come you can do all this other great shit but you can't lie the fuck down and sleep? How come we can't? How can we reconnect with our internal energy signals so that we break the habit of ignoring them? The National Institute of Mental Health has been tracking the growing disparity between women and men in the prevalence of major depression, anxiety, and other debilitating mental health concerns.[20] Women are more stressed, anxious, depressed, angry, and exhausted than their male counterparts, and the very things that are causing them to be more stressed, anxious, depressed, angry, and exhausted are what's keeping them from getting rest.

We need to prioritize getting rest right now, even though we know making the choice to leave something undone can compromise our peace and joy tomorrow. So, rest today, no peace tomorrow, or no rest today with a better chance of peace tomorrow? *This "need rest to feel peace but getting rest now will decrease prospects of peace later" conundrum is what keeps women from resting, not some irrational desire to see how much of a tolerance they can build to sleep deprivation.*

The way out of this conundrum is painfully simple: acknowledge that resting right now will exact a steep price in the near future, acknowledge the price you will pay, make peace with it, and get some rest. We deny ourselves the rest we need so we can prevent the price of chaos/pain/discomfort we believe will follow. But not resting never seems to guarantee rest the next day or the day after that. The denial of rest only seems to trigger a cycle where the more rest you give up, the more rest you will need to continue giving up.

So, just go the fuck to sleep. Deal with the fallout the next day. It won't be pleasant, but it won't be as bad as you imagine. More importantly, you will be rested and in better shape to deal with whatever the fallout is. Right now, we are in a "do, don't rest, do more, don't rest more, do even more" cycle. Let's try the "rest, deal with the fallout, do what we can, rest, deal with the fallout" cycle. Neither cycle feels ideal, but we will be better rested in the latter cycle.

Our phones, our tablets, and our laptops sleep when their batteries are drained. We can watch the battery level going down. We know that when the battery is fully drained, the gadget will shut down, and it will take its time turning back on. When the batteries are dead, the gadget can't borrow from a future charge. If we treated our bodies the same way, we would get the rest we need today.

But we don't have the clearly articulated battery meters that our gadgets do. How can we know when our batteries are about to die? How can we know when to shut down? Here is where we can learn a lot from the art and science of putting toddlers down for a nap.

▷ **Schedule naps and bedtimes.** Our adult bodies, just like our toddler versions, find it harder to sleep when we get overtired. If we don't rest when we first need rest, our brains go into overdrive, and we become hyperactive. We don't have visible battery meters, but our behaviors—especially the behaviors we cannot seem to control—are quite accurate energy meters if we just pay attention to the signs and learn to decipher them accurately. If you find yourself yawning, rubbing your eyes, fidgeting...you need to go the fuck to sleep. If you find yourself reading the same paragraph over and over again, if you are getting cranky...you need to go the fuck to sleep. The best way to avoid the onset of "need rest now" behaviors is to get the rest we need when we need it: Schedule and keep bedtimes and naptimes.

▷ **Make resting places "resty."** Just as our toddlers' minds and bodies absorb environmental cues and triggers for stimulation levels, our adult minds and bodies are equally susceptible to what our environment is telling us to focus on. For example, a bright light in our environment is telling us to be awake and alert, and a darker space with gentle ambient lighting is telling us to close our eyes and rest. If there isn't enough light to read, our brains won't think about reading. If the environment has a lot of sound, we are triggered to listen and process the sounds. Even if we are trying to tune out the sounds, we are actively working to tune out the sounds, and that's not restful. When it's quiet in our environment, we receive the cues to quiet our own minds and bodies. If our computer screens are on, we are cued to interact with our computers. If we see work we need to do, our brains are cued to think about that work. If we see empty surfaces, our brains are cued to empty themselves. Of course, it's not this simple, but it is truer than not. If your resting place isn't "resty," it will be more difficult for you to get the rest you need.

▷ **Check in with your body frequently with quick body scans.** Do a quick body scan four to five times daily. Body scans are great ways for us to get in touch with our inner energy meters. We will learn through these scans where stress likes to sit in our bodies and where tiredness likes to make its home. Do the scans at the end of segments if you are segmenting your day, or schedule them at times when you have to transition from one thing to another, such as leaving your office to go to a meeting or to head home, etc. You can do these scans in your office, in a meeting, in your car, or anywhere else that makes sense for you. You can't do an effective scan if you are moving around or if you are processing a lot of visual, tactile, or audial stimuli in that moment. (A similar scan was described in an earlier chapter; see page 50. That scan is better to create a quick connection to the present moment; this one provides a deeper connection to physical energy.)

BODY SCAN

Sit down and close your eyes if you are comfortable doing so. If not, keep them open, but *focus on a point on the floor and soften your gaze.*

Take a couple of deep breaths and consciously bring your attention to your environment. Where are you? What time is it? What did you just finish doing? What are you going to be doing in the near future?

Bring your attention to your body. Notice how you are sitting, feel the weight of your body in the chair, on the floor or wherever you are seated.

Take a few more deep breaths as you just pay attention to your body. With every inhale, feel your muscles relax a little more and with every exhale feel yourself sink a little deeper into your seat.

Continue to take deep breaths as you start focusing your attention to do a scan.

Bring attention to your feet. Flex your feet up and down. Wiggle your toes.

Move your attention up your calves to your knees. Flex and unflex your calves. Are the muscles tense? Can you soften them a little?

Move from your knees to your thighs and your hips. Is there any tightness there? Can you wiggle around as you sit to loosen the tension? If there is a particularly tight or painful area, can you put your hands on that area for a few seconds before you move on?

Focus on your back and your shoulders. Roll your shoulders a bit. Pay attention to small and big aches in your back and shoulders. Put your hands on particularly tense areas for a few seconds.

Bring your attention down into your stomach area. If your stomach is tense or tight, let it soften, and shrug your shoulders to make your torso generally loosen.

Let your focus move up through your torso and down your arms and into your hands. Shrug your shoulders again if there is tightness in your arms. Flex your hands and wiggle your fingers. Make a fist and release it.

Focus on your neck and jaw. Breathe as deeply as you can. Relax your jaw by touching your tongue to the roof of your mouth. Smile widely and release the smile. Raise your eyebrows and lower them. Soften the muscles in your face as much as possible.

Take your focus inside and do a quick scan of what's in your mind. Notice the thoughts. You don't have to do anything with them right now.

Do a quick review of your body from the top of your head to your toes and back. As you scan, think about what your body needs. Does it need to be hydrated?

Nourished with food? Exercised? Rested? Ask your body what it needs right now.

Thank your body for all that it does every day. Take a few more deep breaths and open your eyes or refocus your gaze.

Stretch your arms above your head. Stand up. Shake your body a little. Think about what your body asked of you and give it what it needs as soon as possible.

Onward!

RECHARGE
Power-Saving Mode

I'm not lazy. I'm in Power Saving Mode.
—Unknown

Humans don't have an objective mechanism for understanding the finiteness of our energy on any given day or for measuring how much energy we have left for that day at any particular moment. And when we do encounter the limit of our energy, we think of it as a weakness or a character flaw, instead of as an essential aspect of our human experience. We celebrate people who ignore these limits, even at their own peril, and we label people who acknowledge these limits lazy and unmotivated.

All humans struggle with objectively measuring our finite energies and our relationships with the limits of those finite energies, but women are particularly bad at acknowledging the finiteness of our energy and accepting its limits.

Samuel Adams has been cited as saying, "It does not take a majority to prevail...but rather an irate, tireless minority, keen on setting brushfires of freedom in the minds of men." I get it, Sam, but honestly, setting brushfires of freedom in the minds of men sounds tiring. Necessary, sure, but exhausting. Similarly, Bishop T.D. Jakes exalts his mother in glowing terms: "My mother worked tirelessly to give my brother, sister, and me every advantage she could, and while her income was modest, she never let that stop her from trying to expand our minds, our worlds or our experiences to help us grow into the best people we could possibly be." That's a beautiful sentiment, but I want to challenge that she did it tirelessly as a black woman in the American South in the '50s and '60s. I am willing to bet that she did it tiredly, not tirelessly, and we should celebrate the hell out of the fact that she did it tiredly.

We use the word *tirelessly*—and its slightly less popular cousins *indefatigably, unflaggingly, inexhaustibly, painstakingly, unflinchingly*, and others, as compliments of the highest order, as badges of honor to demonstrate our admiration and gratitude. However, every time we use these words, we project and reify that being tired, fatigued, or exhausted are weaknesses to be overcome. We are not supposed to flinch or feel pain when we keep going as if our energy is infinite.

What if it wasn't a compliment to say *tirelessly*? What if, instead, the compliment was that a tired, exhausted, and flagging minority set brushfires of freedom in the minds of men in spite of the fact that they were tired, exhausted, and flagging. What if the compliment were that a mother was tired, exhausted, and in pain from working to give her children all she could, and she kept at it anyway?

In praising tirelessness, we dismiss and perhaps even dishonor the tiredness. When we dismiss the tiredness, we make it harder for people to remember that our energy is finite. To be in charge of our lives, we have to acknowledge that we are damn tired when we are damn tired without fear of being perceived as lazy, undedicated, lacking passion, blah, blah, blah.

We have to understand that our energy is finite and that we need to go into Power-Saving Mode when we are starting to run out of energy so that our batteries don't die. It takes less energy to recharge in Power-Saving Mode than it does if your battery has completely died.

When one of our tech gadgets goes into Power-Saving Mode, it hasn't turned itself off quite yet, but it won't do everything it could do if it had more juice. What if we could schedule a couple of hours a day of Power-Saving Mode for ourselves? During this time, it might not be possible to take a nap or shut your brain down completely, but you would only be able to do a limited number of things. Maybe you couldn't do calls or meetings, or maybe you couldn't lead calls or meetings. Maybe you could do that busy work that never seems to get done or you could go grocery shopping.

Depending on your personality, your interests, and your particular work and life demands, your Power-Saving Mode may look very different than someone else's. Whatever you decide it looks like, scheduling a Power-Saving Mode block of an hour or two once or twice a day is a strategy that can neutralize the perception that your energy is infinite and that ignoring your exhaustion and pain somehow makes you a hero.

When in Power-Saving Mode:

▷ **Choose single-tasking over multi-tasking.**

Multitasking is merely the opportunity
to screw up more than one thing at a time.
—*Gary Keller*

Multi-tasking does not make us more productive; it only makes us *feel* more productive. Multi-tasking is an addictive, vicious cycle that exhausts our brain and makes us less efficient while fooling us into thinking that we are being productive when we are just being busy. One of the reasons that we are so wrong about our multi-tasking capabilities is that we conflate multi-tasking with multi-processing. A simple way to think about the difference between tasking and processing is that our unconscious brain can execute on tasks, but our conscious brain needs to be involved in processing.

Our conscious brains are single-processing systems that thrive when they are singularly focused. Our unconscious brains can carry out tasks that don't require our conscious brain's processing power. For example, tasks such as walking, listening to music, driving a familiar route, brushing our teeth, and engaging in other habitual patterns can be executed by our unconscious brains. Processes such as listening to someone, thinking through a problem, composing an email, reading a book, and other complex processes requires that deliberate thinking of the conscious brain.

So, yes, we can multi-task—we can walk and listen to music and chew gum all at the same time—but we can't multi-process. We can't pay attention on a conference call and read emails at the same time. When we try to multi-process, we spend more energy trying to make our brains work in ways that aren't natural, and we are more likely to make mistakes.

You can walk and have a conversation with someone. You can listen to music and clean up emails that you don't need to read too closely. You can read a book and ride a stationary bike. You can chew your food and respond to someone's text. But you can't have a conversation with someone and respond to a text at the same time. You will either miss something that was said, or you will make a mistake in your text.

You can multi-task, but you cannot multi-process, and when you need to go into Power-Saving Mode, it is best to neither multi-process nor multi-task.

Focus on only one thing at a time to conserve energy and soothe your brain. You can always go back to multi-tasking and multi-processing when you are out of Power-Saver Mode!

▷ **Choose easy over difficult.**

Better learn balance.
Balance is key.
—*Mr. Miyagi, The Karate Kid*

It's impossible to make it into adulthood in modern society without hearing and absorbing the message "no pain, no gain." What we don't hear in equal measure is that if there is only pain, there is no gain either. There is no pithy equivalent of "no rest, no gain" to balance the message of "no pain, no gain."

Think of the message that these words by Teddy Roosevelt convey, "Nothing in the world is worth having or worth doing unless it means effort, pain, difficulty...I have never in my life envied a human being who led an easy life." We hold up messages like this to encourage hard work and resilience, but without the balance of a "after hard work, you have to rest" message, resting or slowing down at any point has become equated with laziness and listlessness.

Yes, we need to go the fuck to sleep, to let ourselves rest. But resting when we have depleted all of our energy isn't the answer either. We have to manage our energy during the course of the day by going into Power-Saving Mode, and in this mode, we need to single-task as much as possible, and we need to limit those tasks to things that are easy for us. These are things that are still necessary for us to do, but it's the stuff that doesn't require as much cognitive and/or emotional energy as other stuff.

For example, responding to a routine email about scheduling or a funny email from a friend can be put in the easy zone, but responding to a difficult email from a client or colleague that requires a lot of thought and nuance cannot. Creating an outline for something you need to write may go in the easy zone, but finalizing a document may not. Sorting through your mail may go in the easy zone, but paying the bills may not.

You don't have to know right now what does and does not go in your easy zone. An easy (pun intended!) way to choose easy when in Power-Saving Mode: If it feels hard, stop doing it.

RESET
CTRL+ALT+DEL

Resetting allows you to lead yourself
back to your natural energy.
—Mette Muller

Going into Power-Saving Mode is a great option, letting you at least slow down if you can't fully rest. If you can't slow down, and you don't like the way your day is going or how your energy is feeling, it may be useful to reset before you move forward. Starting with the moment we wake up every morning, we consciously and unconsciously absorb vibes and messages from the world around us. Sometimes we even import vibes from the previous day that we haven't yet processed or resolved. Over the course of our days, these vibes and messages sit in the back of our minds, taking up physical, cognitive, and emotional energies and slowing us down as we work on what needs to get done that day.

Our computers have a convenient reset function—CTRL+ALT+DEL—that pauses the operating system so that the system can clear unneeded processes and reactivate only what is needed. When we feel as if our thoughts are obscured in murky waters or we find our brains flooded with worries about things that aren't connected to the present moment, we can reset just like our technology devices do.

▷ **The Reset Scream(s)**
Before humans had words, we had screams, and now, even after we have created language, we scream when language cannot express the overwhelmingness of what we are feeling. We scream to express many emotions and experiences—pain,

anger, fear, joy, sadness, frustration. The common thread connecting our screams is that we are reacting to what we are feeling with the deepest and most primal part of our brain. This part of our brain does not have language and does not think before it reacts.

We scream unconsciously in reaction to something, but we can also scream deliberately to purge our emotions and reset our brains. Screaming deliberately is different than screaming unconsciously because you are deliberate choosing to activate that primal part of your brain instead of it getting triggered by something out of your control.

When you activate this part of your brain, everything else just kind of stops. All thoughts stop. All emotions stop. The past ceases to exist. You are not worried about your future in that moment. There is just you, in that moment, screaming. This happens because this part of your brain is also responsible for keeping you hyper focused. So, when it is activated, it hijacks all other brain operations until it is satisfied that you don't have to focus as sharply anymore. If you deliberately activate it by screaming, it's still going to hijack your brain in the same way it would if it were triggered by external stimuli.

After you are done screaming, you will have a "coming back" moment in which you have to reorient yourself to where you are, what you were doing, etc. Even if you were having the worst possible day, you don't "come back" from a reset scream with the same emotions and thoughts.

Before you choose this reset mechanism, please make sure that you are in a place where you can scream without freaking out other people. You can also scream into a pillow to muffle the sound.

▷ **The Reset Shake(s)**

Like screaming, shaking is something your body does reactively when it is angry, upset, cold, or uber frustrated. It's an involuntary reaction, but when triggered deliberately, shaking can reset your physical, cognitive, and emotional status quo.

It's more effective to do this while standing, but you can also do it while sitting. Close your eyes, then start with your hands: Just start shaking them. Let the shaking spread up to your shoulders and your neck. Then, shake your hips and legs and toes. What's the difference between shaking, wiggling, or shimmying? Absolutely nothing. Just do whatever comes naturally and do it for two minutes.

If you find yourself thinking about how you are shaking or thinking about anything, shake to one full song and sing along with the lyrics to focus your brain on the present moment. If the song has the word *shake* in it, that's even better for reminding your brain what you are trying to do. There are hundreds of songs with the word *shake* in them, and that's not a coincidence. There is something about shaking that makes us disconnect with everything and reset.

People who like using this reset tactic have recommended several songs that work for them. I have included some of the cleaner ones below. You can try one of them or use any other song that inspires you to shake and sing.

- ▷ *"Shake Your Body (Down to the Ground)" by The Jacksons featuring Michael Jackson*
- ▷ *"Shake It Off" by Taylor Swift*
- ▷ *"Shake Your Groove Thing" by Peaches & Herb*

▷ *"Shake It" by Metro Station*
▷ *"Shake It Up" by Selena Gomez*

▷ **The Reset Song(s)**

Just as music is effective in assisting with a reset scream, it is also effective in quick resets between segments. If you want to use music to create reset moments between segments of your day or after a particularly stressful meeting or call, it can be helpful to pick one song and play it whenever you want to reset. It doesn't matter what the song is, but faster rhythms are more effective than slower beats. After you play that song a few times, your brain will associate that song with a reset, and it will become more and more effective as a reset song with every play.

RESTART
Power Down & Restart (With Updates)

Almost everything will work again
if you unplug it for a few minutes...even you.
—Anne Lamott

It can be annoying as heck when your computer or phone suddenly shuts down because it needs to update, but those updates are often necessary security or other operational fixes that allow the technology to function better, to operate smarter than it did before.

Every day, we learn lessons—some big and some small—about who we are, what we like, what we don't like, who we like, who we don't like, etc. Learning the lessons, however, does not mean that we integrate the lessons into how we operate. Our brains love the predictable routine of the status quo, so they will ignore the lessons until the status quo feels bad enough to motivate us to change. The poem, "Autobiography in Five Chapters," by Portia Nelson, illustrates this poignantly and powerfully:

Autobiography in Five Chapters
by Portia Nelson

I

I walk down the street.
There is a deep hole in the sidewalk
I fall in.
I am lost...
I am hopeless.
It isn't my fault.
It takes forever to find a way out.

II

I walk down the same street.
There is a deep hole in the sidewalk.
I pretend I don't see it.
I fall in again.
I can't believe I'm in the same place.
But it isn't my fault.
It still takes a long time to get out.

III

I walk down the same street.
There is a deep hole in the sidewalk.
I see it is there.
I still fall in...it's a habit
My eyes are open; I know where I am;

It is my fault.
I get out immediately.

IV

I walk down the same street.
There is a deep hole in the sidewalk.
I walk around it.

V

I walk down another street.

How many of us stay stuck in Chapter II with something that is making us miserable? We get better and better at climbing out of that hole, and we call that progress because Chapter III is a hard dose of reality we don't always want to experience. But Chapters IV and V? Just wow, right?

Chapter V is the power of being in charge of our lives. The lessons are there to help us to make this choice. But unless we deliberately tell our brains that we want to do it smarter tomorrow, those lessons will collect dust in remote corners of our brains that we don't visit very often.

If we hold ourselves accountable for deliberately seeking the lessons then updating our operating systems, we can get through Chapter III and on to Chapter V in many areas of our lives that drain our energies. Unfortunately, it's not as easy as just saying that we are interested in learning the lessons. We have to reflect on our days, articulate the lessons learned, imagine how our reality will look and feel different if we integrate this lesson, and power down at night with the intention of integrating the lesson (updating our operating system) as we sleep. It's also helpful to write down the lesson learned in the morning and imagine what it would look like if you operated from this updated perspective.

∗ Diana Realizing ∗

Diana and I met by Zoom in late 2021 as I was finishing this book, and she asked me how I was doing. I told her I was good and started asking about her life, her kids, her work, etc. She stopped me and said "I want to know how you are doing. I know you don't like to talk about yourself, but I really want to know how you are doing."

I couldn't find the words to respond to her. It had been one of the toughest years of my life for a lot of different reasons. I had a few people in my life who knew what I had been going through, but Diana was a client. I didn't know how to respond to her.

She noted my silence and said, "I have been realizing a lot of things lately. I am realizing why you are such a good coach on these issues. You let yourself feel other people's pain. And you can only do that if you have gone through a lot yourself. I just want you to know that I get it and I want you to be okay just as much as you want me to be okay."

I didn't trust myself to say anything without crying so I just nodded. She nodded in return and dove into what was going on in her life.

We had a great conversation, and I told her that I was probably going to include this conversation in the book. She laughed and said, "I almost want to ask you to use my real name. Almost."

ONWARD
FELLOW TRAVELERS!

IN CHARGE?

"You're in charge, but don't touch the controls."

Dr. Shannon Lucid, an astronaut since 1979, received the Congressional Space Medal of Honor in 1996 for her groundbreaking work on the Russian space station *Mir*. President Boris Yeltsin also gave her the Russian Order of Friendship Medal, the highest honor conferred upon non-Russians. In recounting her pioneering work on *Mir*, Dr. Lucid recalls how the Russian cosmonauts told her every single time they left the space station to conduct their spacewalks: *You're in charge,* but *don't touch the controls.*

"Charge" is one of the hardest-working words in the English language. We use the word to technically mean everything from responsibility and control (taking charge of something or someone), to restoring the active materials in a storage battery (charging our phones), to electrifying an audience (the fans were charged by the performance), to requiring payment (charging for a product), to recording an owed debt (charging a credit card) to rushing forward toward something (the bull charged the matador) to ascribing blame (charged with a crime) to understanding the chemistry/physics of matter (negatively charged ions) to name just a few of its various meanings in our everyday parlance.

As women told me the ins and outs of managing their lives and their energy levels, the idea of "Who *is* in charge?" kept emerging as a central theme for how women navigate the world around them. A quick search of books about being in charge reveals titles like *You're in Charge—Now What?: The 8 Point Plan*; *How to Lead When You're Not in Charge: Leveraging Influence When You Lack Authority*; *In Charge: Finding the Leader Within You*; and *Getting Things Done When You Are Not in Charge*—all written by men. And, of course, there is *A Woman in Charge*, a book about Hillary Clinton, also written by a man.

There is an undercurrent of not being "in charge" that animates our public and private lives. This undercurrent, unfortunately, is deeply rooted in the reality that women are not, in fact, in charge of the gears that operate our political and socioeconomic realities. We know this because we live it every day, but the data backs up our experiences.

The World Economic Forum's 2020 Global Gender Gap Report informs us that women occupy roughly 25% of political positions globally, and the gender gap in economic participation will take those in charge about 257 years to close (that's actually worse than the 202 years reported in 2019). The report also reminds us that the one globally consistent thing in the global economy is that there "is no country where men spend the same amount of time on unpaid work [caring for children/families, housework, volunteer work, etc.] as women. In countries where the ratio is lowest, it is still 2:1."

Out of the 153 countries ranked in this global study, the United States is fifty-third overall and in the "bottom half of the global league table for gender equality in the political sphere, trailing behind, for example, the Philippines, India, South Korea, and the United Arab Emirates." In the US, we talk in idiomatic cliches like "motherhood and apple pie" as the things that we all agree are inarguably good; however, the US is in fact one of the most dangerous places in the developed world to become a mother. If motherhood and apple pie go together, apple pie can't be that good for women either.

The Global Gender Gap Report lays out America's reality that while maternal mortality has declined throughout the developed world, "the U.S. rates more than doubled since 1987." What those numbers mean is that about 20 women out of 100,000 die giving birth every year—we went up from 9 to 20 since 1987. In comparison, the UK and Germany have brought their numbers down over the past 30 years; today most developed countries are where we were in the 1980s, while we have regressed rapidly. The situation is especially serious for Black women, who are three to four times more likely to die from childbirth complications than white women."

Oh, and we are one of the very few developed countries that has never had a female head of state.

The "not in charge" discussion doesn't end there, though. It mutates into a "would be funny if it wasn't so not funny" meme when you consider that U.S. companies have more CEOs named John (5.3%), James (5%), and David (4.5%) than they do all women combined (4.1%). The global version includes the not-so-funny reality that in the U.K., there are more CEOs of Financial

Times Stock Exchange companies named Peter than there are female CEOs. The Australian version combines the U.S. and U.K. name games and boosts Johns and Peters to be 40% more likely to end up as CEO than a woman of any name.

It would be funny if it weren't so not funny.

The reality is that when you are not in charge, you are more vulnerable than those who are in charge, especially in volatile times. Consider that since "February 2020 [in the US], women have lost over 6.1 million jobs...This accounts for more than half of the overall job losses since the start of the Covid-19 crisis... women of color have especially [been] hit hard" even though about 41% of mothers in the U.S. are the "are the sole or primary breadwinners in their family, meaning that a woman's salary is essential to meeting the needs of those closest to her."

Close to 20% of working mothers have voluntarily left their jobs due to the pandemic in comparison to about 10% of working fathers. Jessica Grose quotes economist Michael Madowitz in the *New York Times*: "Just before the pandemic hit, for the first time ever, for a couple months, we had more women employed than men. And now we are back to late 1980s levels of women in the labor force."[21] The economic impact of this on women is undeniable, but the overwhelming stress faced by women is nothing short of a mental health crisis—a pandemic inside a pandemic—in our country.

We keep getting the message that we aren't in charge, but we are also told that those in charge are definitely doing it wrong. As McKinsey Consulting so eloquently opines, "Given trends we have observed over the past few months, in a gender-regressive scenario in which no action is taken to counter these effects, we estimate that global GDP growth could be $1 trillion lower in 2030 than it would be if women's unemployment simply tracked that of men in each sector. (It is important to note that the impact could be more severe than the one we have modeled here if factors such as increased childcare burdens, attitudinal bias, a slower recovery, or reduced public and private spending on services such as education or childcare make women leave the labor market permanently.)"

In other words: It's bad if the people in charge do it right and it's really bad if they do it wrong. If what's past is truly prologue for what is to come, I don't have much hope for the Johns, Jims, Davids, and Peters of the world turning this around anytime soon.

Now, that's just dealing with our public lives! The signals are clear that we are not in charge in the public spheres of our lives. In our private lives, the signals are a bit murkier. Like Dr. Lucid, we are told we are in charge, but we are definitely not allowed to touch the controls.

There are hundreds of ways, big and small, through which women receive the message that we are not in charge. This book explores many of these ways in greater detail, but during the COVID-19 pandemic, the experiences of mothers during the various phases of quarantine profoundly reflected how women experience the world around us differently than our male counterparts.

In January 2021, almost a year into the COVID-19 pandemic, the *New York Times* published a series of articles entitled The Primal Scream. The newspaper set up a phone line for mothers to call into to express their day-to-day frustrations, big and small, and found that "hundreds responded with shouts, cries, guttural yells, and lots and lots of expletives." The series, representing the "messy, heartbreaking moments of everyday fear and chaos," hoped to be the public primal scream of the millions of private screams, both uttered and repressed, of working moms. I screamed after reading the first and second articles in the series, "America's Mothers Are in Crisis: Is Anyone Listening to Them?" and "Three American Mothers, On the Brink."

After reading the third article, I screamed again. Aptly entitled "How Society Has Turned Its Back on Mothers: This Isn't Just about Burnout, It's about Betrayal," the article delves into how women are not just burning out because of too much to do; they are burned out because society is failing them. Dr. Pooja Lakshmin, the author and a psychiatrist who specializes in women's mental health, distinguishes between women being burned out and women being betrayed: "'Betrayal' describes what my patients are feeling exactly. While burnout places the blame (and thus the responsibility) on the individual and tells working moms they aren't resilient enough, betrayal points directly to the broken structures around them."

In other words, working moms are being told: "You are in charge of how you work while parenting, but don't touch the controls of how your work life or parenting is defined, supported, acknowledged, or valued." Dr. Lakshmin's first piece of advice to working moms is "to remind yourself that the reason you feel guilty, apathetic, and exhausted during this worldwide crisis is due to choices that were made by people other than yourself. You can't remedy a lack of national pandemic policy or the failure of employers to effectively support families."

I reached out to dozens of leaders for their thoughts on this issue. I didn't hear much from the Johns, Jims, Davids, and Peters, although I want to believe that even if their immediate family circles are inured from this screaming, they could not possibly escape the echoes that were vibrating through every corner of society unless they were actively not listening. As the pandemic dragged on, and women kept screaming literally and metaphorically, it didn't seem like many people who could touch the controls were actually listening.

As women bump up against the controls in their private lives that they are not allowed to touch, we are rethinking what it means to be in charge of our lives. We are manipulating the only controls we are being allowed to—we are resigning from our jobs (The Great Take This Job And Shove It Resignation), we are reassessing family dynamics, we are raising our children with grace and grit while being chastised for not taking better care of ourselves, we are finding ways to take better care of ourselves in spite of the obstacles in our way, and we are insisting that workplaces cannot go back to the ways of old when we now know that we can work differently. Through our screams and the jagged edges of how we are making decisions today, we are revealing how much the workings of the world have never worked for us.

So, what do we do to move forward? We could continue working our butts off to get more women into positions of power and hold organizations of all types accountable for advancing gender equity, but the positive return on investment on that effort has been marginal at best and only for the most incremental of changes. Yes, that's an option, but it will take too long, and the whisper of "you're in charge, but don't touch the controls" is ever present in how women are treated when we sit right next to or even replace a John, Jim, David, or Peter.

Of course, we want the badass women who are in positions of leadership, like Kamala Harris, Janet Yellen, Nancy Pelosi, Kathrin Jansen, Melinda Gates, Oprah Winfrey, Shonda Rhimes, Alexandria Ocasio-Cortez, Christine Lagarde, Cynthia Marshall, Mary Barra, Sonia Sotomayor, Jacinda Ardern, Katrín Jakbsdóttir, Serena Williams, Radhika Jones, Michelle Obama, Beyoncé, and others to change the world from their influential positions, but we also know that they face their own challenges being in those leadership positions. So, yes, badass women leaders, do what you can do!

Let's influence change where we can—and let's also acknowledge that meaningful changes aren't flowing to the majority of women right now.

Alternatively, we could teach women how to survive and succeed in these strongholds of male dominance, but we've tried that, and honestly, it has only made women infinitely more miserable with very little gain to offset the misery. For example, studies show that success in politics or business "leads to a higher risk of divorce for women" but "makes no difference for men."[22] And (motherhood and apple pie trope alert!) not only is the U.S. becoming more dangerous for women who are giving birth to children, it is growing more challenging for women who want to have successful careers and children. As Sylvia Ann Hewitt warned us almost 20 years ago:

> There is a secret out there—a painful, well-kept secret: At midlife, between a third and a half of all successful career women in the United States do not have children. In fact, 33% of such women (business executives, doctors, lawyers, academics, and the like) in the 41-to-55 age bracket are childless—and that figure rises to 42% in corporate America. These women have not chosen to remain childless. The vast majority, in fact, yearn for children. Indeed, some have gone to extraordinary lengths to bring a baby into their lives. They subject themselves to complex medical procedures, shell out tens of thousands of dollars, and derail their careers—mostly to no avail, because these efforts come too late. In the

words of one senior manager, the typical high-achieving woman childless at midlife has not made a choice but a "creeping nonchoice."[23]

Perhaps we could change our names to John, Jim, David, or Peter and test the edges of that statistical probability.

Or we could disrupt and transform the definition of being in charge in a way that makes sense for us, the badass women who navigate the freedoms, the constrictions, the expectations, the limitations, the celebrations, the pain, the successes, and the disappointments of life with equal parts grace, joy, anger, and exhaustion. We want to fix the societal shit for sure, but we also just don't want to be this damn tired at the end of every day. We aren't asking to do less work, but we do want less shit clogging up our abilities to laugh, chill, love, and dance our way through our days. We want the right to get help when we get sick from all the shit without being told that we would get better if we just quit our jobs and stop trying to have it all. And we want to stop feeling like if we are caught laughing, chilling, loving, and dancing, we can't possibly be doing all the work that we are supposed to be getting done as a woman.

What if we were to define what being in charge looks like? What if we had more options available to us than we realize?

If 2020 and 2021 taught us nothing else, they taught us that when enough people do something differently, the old norms explode to accommodate the new behaviors and new unpredictable norms become our new reality instantaneously. Women's initiatives and advocates for women's advancement have been pushing for years to allow more remote work opportunities because it would make it easier for women, especially working moms, to balance their multiple responsibilities. Leaders resisted in every way possible. When COVID-19 came along and working remotely was the only option available, even for leaders, Zoom became the new norm. When the people in charge had to work from home, working from home became the new norm.

We, the badass women, can surf this sudden shift in norms and radically transform what it means to be in charge. When I was pregnant with my son, I was hospitalized for the last two months of my pregnancy. My daughter was 16 months old, and between not being able to see her every day and being bed bound with no fresh air for weeks, I broke down in tears one day. My nurse, Mia, a quiet older woman who had barely spoken to me until then, said in a soft but steady voice, "well, when shit falls apart, the universe is just saving you the trouble of having to break it apart." She smiled and went about her work as if she hadn't just said one of the most profound things I've ever heard in my life. I asked her what she meant, and she said that whenever things fell apart in her life, she asked herself whether what was falling apart was something she would have wanted to break anyway. And, if she found even one thing she would have broken anyway, she considered the situation a time- and energy-saving endeavor that was happening for her, not to her. (A badass woman, right?) Her advice reminded me of an old Norse saying: *Don't try to fix what we should break before it breaks us.*

What if we have been trying to fix things that we should have been breaking because they were breaking us? What if we look at everything that is broken for women right now and ask ourselves what we would have wanted to break by choice anyway? What if we look around the chaos we are mired in right now and ask what it would look like if we walked into the future redefining what being in charge meant to us? As the business coach Helen Harkness says, "Chaos breeds creativity. Chaos destroys the familiar. It is the bedrock that moves you forward creatively into your future." What would it look like to use this chaos to create something new, something that works *for* us instead of breaking us?

I asked my friend Darla this question, and she told me that being in charge from this point forward meant that she would "never put on heels again, for anything, ever." I asked her how she could start making it happen. She took all her high-heeled shoes, put them in a garbage bag, took them outside, and threw them in the trash. She went back outside five minutes later, took the bag out of the trash, and put it in her garage because "okay, some of those shoes were really expensive, and they don't need to be in my closet but maybe not in the trash yet. Baby steps."

We talked about the fact that she would have wanted to break that norm of "heels=sophisticated" even if the pandemic hadn't come along. Those heels in her closet were a reminder that she was not in charge, that she had to bend (her feet and toes literally) to norms not of her choosing. It didn't mean she would never want to wear heels, but if she wore heels, it would be because she wanted to, not because she had to. A simple act of being in charge for her was choosing what she put on her feet.

One of my colleagues, Kim, had unsuccessfully tried to color her hair on her own soon after the pandemic shut down the hair salon where she had been "beating back the grays" for over 20 years. After her botched attempt to color her gray hair, she decided to let "the grays win." "Why is gray hair considered distinguished on men and frumpy on women? I'm done with this." She hasn't dyed her hair since, and her now gorgeous mane of grays and silvers is a daily reminder of her ability to choose what she wants to look like.

When I was brainstorming some ideas for this book with her, she told me that when she decided to not dye her gray hair anymore, she realized that she never remembered making the decision to start dyeing it in the first place. "It was just a given when I started seeing gray hairs that I would try and hide them. I don't remember ever making a conscious decision about coloring my grays, so making a conscious decision to stop coloring them made me think about how many other things I had just automatically started doing."

Darla's and Kim's stories reminded me of something that Alicia Keys (a badass woman for sure!) wrote in 2016 when she stopped wearing makeup. I cannot possibly summarize her powerful words adequately, so I included an excerpt from her Lenny Letter below[24]:

> I was finally uncovering just how much I censored myself, and it scared me. Who was I anyway? Did I even know HOW to be brutally honest anymore? Who I wanted to be? I didn't know the answers exactly, BUT I desperately wanted to. In one song I wrote, called "When a Girl Can't Be Herself" it says, "In the morning from the minute that I wake up/What if I don't want to put on all that makeup/Who says I must conceal what I'm made of/Maybe all this Maybelline is covering my self-esteem..."
>
> Time passed after I wrote "When a Girl Can't Be Herself," and I didn't think about it much...It wasn't until I walked into one of my first shoots for my new album recently that the issue was front and center again. I'd just come from the gym, had a scarf under my baseball cap, and the beautiful photographer Paola (never met a Paola I didn't like) said, "I have to shoot you right now, like this! The music is raw and real, and these photos have to be too!"

I was shocked. Instantly, I became a bit nervous and slightly uncomfortable. My face was totally raw. I had on a sweatshirt! As far as I was concerned, this was my quick run-to-the-shoot-so-I-can-get-ready look, not the actual photo-shoot look. So, I asked her, "Now?! Like right now? I want to be real, but this might be too real!!" And that was it. She started to shoot me. It was just a plain white background, me and the photographer intimately relating, me and that baseball hat and scarf and a bunch of invisible magic circulating. And I swear it is the strongest, most empowered, most free, and most honestly beautiful that I have ever felt. Once the photo I took with Paola came out as the artwork for my new song "In Common," it was that truth that resonated with others who posted #nomakeup selfies in response to this real and raw me."

I was confused when I first read this. What did it mean for a performer of her stature to not wear makeup? Would it even last? I recognized immediately that my questions were rooted in my disbelief that she could change the rules of how women were supposed to look and present themselves. I followed her #nomakeup journey for a while before it finally hit me that she wasn't changing the rules. She was breaking them because they weren't working for her.

The stories above reflect the most basic of contexts in which women realized that they could be in charge of their own lives—shoes, hair, makeup. The context is basic, but the act of reclaiming your right to decide for yourself what you want to look like is quite profound. It's just a beginning, but what a powerful beginning it is that women are rethinking the rules around how we are physically supposed to look.

I sure was not invited to that meeting where it was decided that high heels were more sophisticated than flats, gray hair was not acceptable, and makeup was mandatory to look polished. Yes, we can try and change these rules that we didn't have a part in creating, or we can just decide not to follow them. ***If enough of us just started doing it differently, could the rules still survive?***

I do realize how utterly idealistic and perhaps even unrealistic that sounds. Even as I write this, the professional and personal costs of such blasphemy are running through my mind and making me want to delete the sentences and write something more...reasonable. At the same time, I wonder if now—in the wake of the pandemic's various disruptions—is not somehow the perfect time to have these conversations and to challenge what we ever meant by reasonable.

What if we collectively stopped trying to change the rules and just had a blast breaking them? We could break all the rules that don't work for us, that drain our energy, until the aggregate of the micro-rebellions changes our world for good.

Darla is breaking the rules on heels...for herself. Kim is breaking the rules on gray hair...for herself. Alicia Keys is breaking the rules on makeup...for herself. Tammy Duckworth, the first sitting senator to give birth while in office (I love when people phrase it like that, as if nearly all senators in history were actually capable of giving birth while in office!), is breaking the rules on babies being allowed on the Senate floor by bringing her newborn with her and breastfeeding her when she needed to. (The Senate did hurry up and pass a bill "allowing" breastfeeding so that Senator Duckworth wouldn't be breaking the rules, but she was pretty clear that she was going to do what she wanted regardless of whether the rules changed or not.) Women like Beyoncé, Meghan

Markle, and Chrissy Teigen are breaking the rules on talking about miscarriages because they've decided that the rules of being silent to make everyone else comfortable are less important than taking care of themselves and their families.

And, when each of these women breaks the rules—rules they had no part in creating—for themselves, they are taking charge of their own experiences, and they are making it easier for other women to break the rules after them. They are weakening the structures that make it possible for the rules to exist. They are making it harder and harder for the rules to survive.

This transformation of being in charge is not always easy or linear or predictable, but I've seen it change people's lives in small but meaningful ways. Some of these transformations were not always by choice, but as Nurse Mia taught me, if there is an aspect of what's falling apart that you would have wanted to break anyway, usher the change in with a smile. *Being in charge is not about trying to get into positions of power; it's remembering that we already have the power to do more than we allow ourselves to do. We are already in the most important position of power of all—being able to choose the who, what, when, where, and why of our badass lives.* And, when enough women start exercising this power daily, the norms of what it means to be in power will change.

She remembered who she was,
and the game changed.
—Lalah Delia

Touch All the Controls

The most common way people give up their power
is by thinking they don't have any.
—Alice Walker

The Boston Marathon did not officially let women compete until 1972, but a woman ran and almost won in 1967. Kathrine Switzer registered for the race as K. V. Switzer, and she captures her dramatic experience on April 19, 1967, in her memoir *Marathon Woman*:

> As we jogged over to the start, Tom [Switzer's boyfriend who was also a marathon runner] said, "God, you're wearing lipstick!"
> "I always wear lipstick. What's wrong with that?"
> "Somebody might see you are a girl and not let you run. Take it off."
> "I will not take off my lipstick."
> And that's how we arrived at the start.

Switzer wrote movingly about her experiences during the race, from the first few miles ("[t]he running is easy, the crowd noise is exciting, and your companions are conversational and affable") to the first moment she knew she'd been spotted and sensed trouble—when a man in a hat and overcoat appeared, in the middle of the road, near Mile 4. He reached for her hand and tried to speak to her, but she was able to maneuver around him and continue on. As she passed, she realized he was a race official.

Just seconds later, she heard footsteps—not the soft rubber running-shoe footsteps of the other athletes, but the distinct sound of leather dress shoes, gaining ground behind her. Switzer registered the sound as dangerous, "an alien and alarming sound" that caused her to turn. She saw *the most vicious face I'd ever seen. A big man, a huge man, with bared teeth was set to pounce, and before I could react he grabbed my shoulder and flung me back, screaming, "Get the hell out of my race and give me those numbers!" Then he swiped down my front, trying to rip off my bib number, just as I leapt backward from him. He missed the numbers, but I was so surprised and frightened that I slightly wet my pants and turned to run. But now the man had the back of my shirt and was swiping at the bib number on my back...*

Switzer was terrified, and frozen. The man had grabbed on to her shirt. Just as suddenly, her boyfriend launched a cross-body block, and sent the man flying onto the side of the road.

This brought a new dilemma: Switzer wondered if she should step off the course, rather than create a larger incident and risk upending the race. But just as quickly, she thought better of it:

I knew if I quit, nobody would ever believe that women had the capability to run 26-plus miles. If I quit, everybody would say it was a publicity stunt. If I quit, it would set women's sports back, way back, instead of forward. If I quit, I'd never run Boston. If I quit, Jock Semple [the race official who attacked Switzer during the race] and all those like him would win. My fear and humiliation turned to anger.

And so she persisted. She began to run again, settling back into the rhythm that would carry her the rest of the 26.2 miles. But there was one more memorable incident ahead of her.

When her boyfriend, Tom, caught up with her he was fuming mad. He had Olympic aspirations, and now he worried that his athletic career was over because he'd hit an official. "You're getting me in all kinds of trouble!" he blurted at her. He ripped his race bib from his chest, threw it to the ground, and shouted at her, "I am never going to make the Olympic team and it's all your fault." And then, slipping away, he hissed, "Besides that, you run too slow anyway." He took off running, disappearing into the field of runners ahead, and left her behind, all alone. She wrote

> I couldn't help it. I felt so ashamed, I was crying. Again Tom had convinced me I was just a girl, a jogger, and a no-talent like me now had bumbled the Olympic Dream out of his life. I thought I was a serious girlfriend to him, and so I guessed that was over, too. It was a helluva race so far, that's for sure, and we still had over 20 miles to run.

She made it across the finish line. Back then, marathons weren't the spectacle they are today, with thousands lining the racecourse and thousands more at the finish. Switzer and the male runners were greeted by perhaps a dozen people, one of whom covered her with an army blanket. A handful of reporters asked a few desultory questions ("What made you do it? Why Boston? Are you a suffragette?") and then Switzer was left alone.

Switzer did not win the Boston Marathon in 1967, but the newspaper coverage of her dramatic experience and finish ensured that, contrary to popular opinion at the time, women would not pass out within 1500 meters of a race.

She was told she could not run. She ran. She was attacked by one of the race organizers during the race. She survived and finished.

I don't know what Dr. Shannon Lucid did when the Russian cosmonauts told her that she was "in charge" but to "not touch the controls." I imagine she touched all the controls she needed to because she was honored for her pioneering work by both the United States and by Russia.

We are constantly told what we cannot or should not do as women, but we have the power to do it anyway.

Exercise the power.

Touch all the controls.

Enjoy the ride.

> *If you obey all the rules, you miss all the fun.*
> —*Katherine Hepburn*

ENJOY ALL THE MOMENTS

You only live once, but if you do it right, once is enough.
—*Mae West*

This life is complex, messy, chaotic, unfair, exhausting. This life is also fun, peaceful, beautiful, amazing, and worth it. We only live once, but we do have the power to do it right. Let's live this life in whatever way feels right for us, and peace, joy, acknowledgment, and community will follow.

We don't need to get in charge.

We are already in charge.

Onward!

Endnotes

1 All of these can be characteristics of exhaustion and burnout, but they can also be symptoms of more serious mental health issues that require more than just energy management strategies. The strategies in this book are not a substitute for necessary therapeutic interventions. As women, we are sometimes quick to believe that we can power through anything, but we cannot power through everything. Talk to a physician, a therapist, or other professionals about your mental health even as you experiment with ideas in this book. One critical thing that writing this book has taught me is that we need all the things that help us!

2 https://www.who.int/news/item/28-05-2019-burn-out-an-occupational-phenomenon-international-classification-of-diseases

3 https://www.mckinsey.com/featured-insights/diversity-and-inclusion/for-mothers-in-the-workplace-a-year-and-counting-like-no-other

4 Megan Leonhardt, "9.8 Million Working Mothers in the U.S. Are Suffering from Burnout," December 3, 2020, CNBC, https://www.cnbc.com/2020/12/03/millions-of-working-mothers-in-the-us-are-suffering-from-burnout.html.

5 Kristin Wong, "There's a Stress Gap Between Men and Women. Here's Why It's Important, New York Times, November 14, 2018, https://www.nytimes.com/2018/11/14/smarter-living/stress-gap-women-men.html.

6 Carlene Boucher, "A Qualitative Study of the Impact of Emotional Labour on Health Managers, TQR, November 29, 2016, https://nsuworks.nova.edu/tqr/vol21/iss11/15/.

7 In this body of psychological research, conative and behavioral are often consolidated into one category. In my interviews with women, I found that conative processes did not always match up with behavioral processes because of conflicts women faced in meeting other people's needs (with immediate negative consequences for not doing so) and meeting their own needs (with delayed negative consequences for not doing so). I analyzed the information from my interviews by using the four as separate processes to better understand how women were making their decisions and what could lead to decisions that would have more positive outcomes.

8 Nikos L.D. Chatzisarantis, Martin Hagger, and Cecilia Thøgersen-Ntoumani, "The Effects of Self-Discordance, Self-Concordance, and Implementation Intentions on Health Behavior, Journal of Applied Behavioral Research, January 2009, 13(4) 198–214, doi:10.1111/j.1751-9861.2008.00035.x.

9 Kennon M. Sheldon and Andrew J. Elliot, Goal Striving, Need Satisfaction, and Longitudinal Well-Being: The Self-Concordance Model, Journal of Personality and Social Psychology, 1999 Vol 76, no 3 482–497. https://selfdeterminationtheory.org/SDT/documents/1999_SheldonElliot.pdf

10 Kirtly Parker Jones, The Scope, podcast audio, February 6, 2014, https://healthcare.utah.edu/the-scope/shows.php?shows=0_vfhu9ewv.

11 Chris Hook, "Partners the Biggest Threat to Women as Sobering Stats Take Centre Stage on International Day for the Elimination of Violence Against Women," 7News, November 25, 2019, https://7news.com.au/news/social/partners-the-biggest-threat-to-women-as-sobering-stats-take-centre-stage-on-international-day-for-the-elimination-of-violence-against-women-c-573365.

12 World Health Organization, "Devastatingly Pervasive: 1 in 4 Women Globally Experience Violence," March 9, 2021, https://www.who.int/news/item/09-03-2021-devastatingly-pervasive-1-in-3-women-globally-experience-violence.

13 Mindi Chahal, "Consumers Less Likely to 'Opt In' to Marketing than 'Opt Out,'" Marketing Week, April 29, 2014, https://www.marketingweek.com/consumers-less-likely-to-opt-in-to-marketing-than-to-opt-out/.

14 Alia E. Dastagir, "The One Word Women Need to Be Saying More Often," USA Today, April 21, 2021, https://www.usatoday.com/story/life/health-wellness/2021/04/20/why-its-so-hard-for-women-to-say-no/7302181002/.

15 Erin Wildermuth, "The Science of Celebration: Five Reasons Organizations Should Do It More Often," Michael Hyatt & Co., https://michaelhyatt.com/science-of-celebration/#:~:text=Celebration%20releases%20happiness&text=That%20is%20endorphins%20in%20action,your%20own%20personal%20motivation%20machine.&text=Depression%20is%20linked%20to%20deficits,reward%2C%20and%20serotonin%20by%20community.

16 Claire Luchette, "The Science of Swearing," Smithsonian Magazine, January 30, 2018, https://www.smithsonianmag.com/science-nature/science-swearing-180967874/.

17 Donovan, James M. and Anderson, H. Edwin, Anthropology and Law. New York: Berghahn Books, 2006.

18 Fouts, Roger S. and Deborah H. Fouts, "Chimpanzees' Use of Sign Language," in The Great Ape Project, eds. Paola Cavalieri and Peter Singer. New York: St. Martin's Griffin, 1993: 28–41, http://www.animal-rights-library.com/texts-m/fouts01.htm.

19 Brian Krans, "Don't Watch Your Mouth. Swearing Can Actually Be Good for Your Health," Healthline, February 3, 2021, https://www.healthline.com/health-news/dont-watch-your-mouth-swearing-can-actually-be-good-for-your-health.

20 National Institutes of Mental Health, "Major Depression," https://www.nimh.nih.gov/health/statistics/major-depression.

21 Jessica Grose, "America's Mothers Are in Crisis," New York Times, February 21, 2021, https://www.nytimes.com/2021/02/04/parenting/working-moms-mental-health-coronavirus.html.

22 Torsten Bell, "Insights...The High Price Successful Working Women Pay," The Guardian, August 25, 2019, https://www.theguardian.com/commentisfree/2019/aug/25/hidden-gems-high-price-successful-working-women-pay.

23 Sylvia Ann Hewlett, "Executive Women and the Myth of Having It All," Harvard Business Review, April 2002, https://hbr.org/2002/04/executive-women-and-the-myth-of-having-it-all.

24 Hairston, "Alicia Keys: Time to Uncover," Lenny, December 8, 2017, https://www.lennyletter.com/story/alicia-keys-time-to-uncover.

Resources

▷ Adams, Samuel.

▷ Ahmed, Mandeq.

▷ Angelou, Maya.

▷ Ardito, Carla Melucci.

▷ Armstrong, Louis. "What a Wonderful World." Written and produced by Bob Thiele. United Recording, 1967.

▷ Bell, Torsten. "Insights...The High Price Successful Working Women Pay," *The Guardian*, August 25, 2019, https://www.theguardian.com/commentisfree/2019/aug/25/hidden-gems-high-price-successful-working-women-pay.

▷ "Bishop T.D. Jakes Shares a Special Mother's Day Message. *Essence*. October 29, 2020. https://www.essence.com/news/bishop-td-jakes-shares-a-special-mothers/

▷ Bunch, Charlotte. *Passionate Politics*. Macmillan, 1987.

▷ Campbell, Joseph.

▷ Chahal, Mindi. "Consumers Less Likely to 'Opt In' to Marketing than 'Opt Out,'" *Marketing Week*, April 29, 2014, https://www.marketingweek.com/consumers-less-likely-to-opt-in-to-marketing-than-to-opt-out/.

▷ Cox, Ida. "Wild Women Don't Have the Blues." Paramount, 1924.

▷ Dastagir, Alia E. "The One Word Women Need to Be Saying More Often," *USA Today*, April 21, 2021, https://www.usatoday.com/story/life/health-wellness/2021/04/20/why-its-so-hard-for-women-to-say-no/7302181002/.

▷ Delia, Lalah.

▷ De Saint-Exupéry, Antoine. *Wind, Sand, and Stars*. Reynal and Hitchcock, 1939.

▷ Donovan, James M. and Anderson, H. Edwin, *Anthropology and Law*. New York: Berghahn Books, 2006.

▷ Doyle, Glennon. *Untamed*. Dial Press, 2020.

▷ Dunne, Peter Finley.

▷ Einstein, Albert.

▷ Estés, Clarissa Pinkola. *Women Who Run with the Wolves: Myths and Stories of the Wild Woman Archetype*. Ballentine Books, 1992.

▷ Ferguson, Jill L. "The Power and Solidarity of Women." March 9, 2017. *HuffPost*. https://www.huffpost.com/entry/the-power-and-solidarity-_b_9410406

▷ Fetell Lee, Ingrid. "Forget Happiness—Pursue Joy: Q & A with Ingrid Fetell Lee. *Goop*, https://goop.com/wellness/mindfulness/forget-happiness-pursue-joy/.

▷ Forgione, Marc.

▷ Fouts, Roger S. and Deborah H. Fouts, "Chimpanzees' Use of Sign Language," in *The Great Ape Project*, eds. Paola Cavalieri and Peter Singer. New York: St. Martin's Griffin, 1993: 28–41, http://www.animal-rights-library.com/texts-m/fouts01.htm.

▷ Grose, Jessica. "America's Mothers Are in Crisis," *New York Times*, February 21, 2021, https://www.nytimes.com/2021/02/04/parenting/working-moms-mental-health-coronavirus.html.

▷ Hairston, "Alicia Keys: Time to Uncover," *Lenny*, December 8, 2017, https://www.lennyletter.com/story/alicia-keys-time-to-uncover.

▷ Gilbert, Elizbeth.

▷ Harkness, Helen.

▷ Harrell, S. Kelley.

▷ Harris, Joanne. *Chocolat*. Penguin, 2000.

▷ Herschel, Abraham Joshua. *The Wisdom of Heschel*. Farrar, Straus and Giroux, 1986.

▷ Hepburn, Katharine.

▷ Hewlett, Sylvia Ann. "Executive Women and the Myth of Having It All." *Harvard Business Review*. April 2002. https://hbr.org/2002/04/executive-women-and-the-myth-of-having-it-all.

▷ Hook, Chris. "Partners the Biggest Threat to Women as Sobering Stats Take Centre Stage on International Day for the Elimination of Violence Against Women," 7News, November 25, 2019, https://7news.com.au/news/social/partners-the-biggest-threat-to-women-as-sobering-stats-take-centre-stage-on-international-day-for-the-elimination-of-violence-against-women-c-573365.

▷ Jefferson, Thomas, et al, July 4, Declaration of Independence. 0704, 1776. Manuscript/Mixed Material. https://www.loc.gov/item/mtjbib000159/.

▷ Jones, Kirtly Parker. *The Scope*, podcast audio, February 6, 2014, https://healthcare.utah.edu/the-scope/shows.php?shows=0_vfhu9ewv.

▷ Joyce, Amy, and Ellen McCarthy. "Working Moms Are Not Okay." *Washington Post*. October 30, 2020.

▷ *Karate Kid*. Written by Robert Mark Kamen, directed by John G. Avildsen, produced by Jerry Weintrab. Columbia Pictures, 1984.

▷ Keller, Gary.

▷ Keller, Helen. Hellen Keller Spiritual Life Center. https://hkslc.org/economic-justice/

▷ Krans, Brian. "Don't Watch Your Mouth. Swearing Can Actually Be Good for Your Health," *Healthline*, February 3, 2021, https://www.healthline.com/health-news/dont-watch-your-mouth-swearing-can-actually-be-good-for-your-health.

▷ Lakshmin, Pooja. "How Society Has Turned Its Back on Mothers." Primal Scream. *New York Times*. February 4, 2021.

▷ Lamott, Anne.

▷ Layne, Erica. The Life on Purpose Movement. https://ericalayne.co/7-ways-to-accept-and-lean-into-a-season-of-rest/rest-is-not-idle-2/

▷ Luchette, Claire. "The Science of Swearing," *Smithsonian Magazine*, January 30, 2018, https://www.smithsonianmag.com/science-nature/science-swearing-180967874/.

▷ Lucid, Shannon.

▷ Mansbach, Adam. *Go the F*ck to Sleep*. Akashic Books, 2011.

▷ Manson, Mark. *The Subtle Art of Not Giving a F*ck: A Counterintuitive Approach*. HarperOne, 2016.

▷ Marsalis, Wynton.

▷ Maxwell, John C. *Developing the Leaders around You: How to Help Others Reach their Full Potential*. HarperCollins, 2005.

▷ May, Kate Torgovnick. "'Women's Friendships Are a Renewable Source of Power': Jane Fonda and Lily Tomlin at TEDWomen 2015." TEDBlog. May 29, 2015. https://blog.ted.com.

▷ McCarthy, Tom. "Albright: 'Special Place in Hell' for Women Who Don't Support Clinton." *The Guardian*. February 6, 2016. https://www.theguardian.com/us-news/2016/feb/06/madeleine-albright-campaigns-for-hillary-clinton.

▷ McGraw, Bill, ed. *The Quotations of Mayor Coleman A. Young*. Wayne State University Press, 2005.

▷ Miranda, Lin Manual. *Hamilton: An American Musical*. Atlantic Records, 2015.

▷ Morissette, Alanis.

▷ Morisson, Toni. *Song of Solomon*. Vintage, 2004.

▷ Muller, Mette.

▷ National Institutes of Mental Health, "Major Depression," https://www.nimh.nih.gov/health/statistics/major-depression.

▷ Nelson, Portia. "Autobiography in Five Short Chapters." Doorway to Self Esteem. https://www.doorway-to-self-esteem.com/autobiography-in-five-short-chapters.html.

▷ Ouimet, Darlene. *Emerging from Broken: The Beginning of Hope for Emotional Healing*. Ebook: http://emergingfrombroken.com/emerging-from-broken-the-beginning-of-hope-for-emotional-healing/

▷ Oxford Dictionary.

▷ Patel, Jyoti.

▷ Picasso, Pablo.

▷ Paycheck, Johnny. "Take this Job and Shove It." *Take this Job and Shove It*. Produced by Billy Sherrill. CBS Recording Studios, 1977.

▷ Pinker, Steven.

▷ Popova, Maria. "Ursula K. LeGuin on the Sacredness of Public Libraries." *The Marginalian*, https://www.themarginalian.org/2015/11/06/ursula-k-le-guin-libraries/.

▷ Roosevelt, Theodore.

▷ *Shar,* Poetic Evolution

▷ Switzer, Kathrine. *Marathon Woman: Running the Race to Revolutionize Women's Sports.* Da Capo Press, 2007.

▷ TerKeurst, Lysa.

▷ Turlington, Christy.

▷ Twain, Mark.

▷ Ulrich, Laurel Thatcher. *Well-Behaved Women Seldom Make History.* Knopf, 2007.

▷ Walker, Alice.

▷ Watson, Emma. "Emma Watson Narrates Powerful Short Film on Gender Equality." September 26, 2016. *EW.* https://ew.com/article/2016/09/26/emma-watson-short-film-gender-equality/.

▷ West, Mae.

▷ Wiest, Brianna. "This Is What Self-Care REALLY Means, Because It's not All Bath Salts and Chocolate Cake. *Thought Catalog.* October 28, 2021. https://thoughtcatalog.com/brianna-wiest/2017/11/this-is-what-self-care-really-means-because-its-not-all-salt-baths-and-chocolate-cake/.

▷ Wildermuth, Erin. "The Science of Celebration: Five Reasons Organizations Should Do It More Often," Michael Hyatt & Co., https://michaelhyatt.com/science-of-celebration/#:~:text=Celebration%20releases%20happiness&text=That%20is%20endorphins%20in%20action,your%20own%20personal%20motivation%20machine.&text=Depression%20is%20linked%20to%20deficits,reward%2C%20and%20serotonin%20by%20community.

▷ World Health Organization. "Burn-Out an 'Occupational Phenomenon': International Classification of Diseases." Health Topics. May 28, 2019.

▷ World Health Organization, "Devastatingly Pervasive: 1 in 4 Women Globally Experience Violence," March 9, 2021, https://www.who.int/news/item/09-03-2021-devastatingly-pervasive-1-in-3-women-globally-experience-violence.

About the author

Mom. Writer. Advocate. Artist. Researcher.
Advisor. Lawyer. Storyteller. Teacher.
Catalyst. Rulebreaker. Student. Reader. Traveler.

Born in India and raised in India, Libya, and Tanzania before arriving in the United States, Arin learned (and forgot and re-learned) several languages before she graduated from high school as an English-speaking adopted native of Chicago. What stayed with her through the experiences of navigating family scattered across many countries, attending schools taught in various languages and traditions, and forging friendships across different cultures was that differences between people weren't challenges to be overcome, they were sources of learning, adventure, and fun. These lessons guided her journeys through the legal profession, academia, and social entrepreneurship.

Arin studied business at DePaul University's College of Commerce, attended law school at University of Southern California, and received her Ph.D. in Sociology from Northwestern University. Arin's research, scholarship and consulting at Nextions, the firm she founded almost 25 years ago, focuses on all aspects of people in workplaces. She has led several ground breaking studies on race/ethnicity, gender, generations, and other differences in workplaces

Her passion for the past few years has been in the areas of wellness and how wellness intersects with inclusion and equity. The research on wellness led her to the research on women and energy management, and this book grew organically from her research and coaching with women on their wellness and energy management.